Last Bus Out

The True Story of Courtney Miles' Rescue of
over 300
People in Hurricane Katrina's Aftermath

by

Beck McDowell

2

Cover Design: Drew McDowell
Story Idea: Emily Elam

3

This story is dedicated to the people of

New Orleans and the Gulf Coast

who still battle depression, fear, anger, and nightmares

in their determination to triumph over great loss.

May their courage be rewarded

and their faith remain strong.

Also available as an Enhanced E-book. See LastBusOut.com.

Contents:

Preface

Epilogue

Afterword

Acknowledgements

6

Preface

main character ↑

illegal

⌐ *This is the true story of Courtney Miles, a boy from the projects with no driver's license and very little driving experience—a boy who gave "taking the bus" a whole new meaning. On a sweltering August day, 2005, while government officials discussed and emailed and planned, Courtney climbed behind the wheel of a school bus and rescued hundreds of people stranded in the aftermath of Hurricane Katrina. He'd spent his entire life trying to stay out of trouble, trying not to repeat the mistakes of his parents, and he knew his ride might land him in jail. But the people he loved needed help. caring*

friend *The friend Courtney took along that day who became a second driver, Jabbar Gibson, received national attention—in newspapers, on blogs, and in nationally televised interviews when his was the first bus to arrive at the Astrodome in Houston. Jabbar told news reporters the police "gave" him the keys to a bus parked at the Superdome.* lied

Courtney kept quiet about the leading role he played in the bus borrowing caper—partly because of his modesty, but also because of his fear that he'd be punished.

Jabbar's story ends like that of many of Courtney's friends from the projects of New Orleans—with an arrest by federal narcotics agents on charges of cocaine and heroin trafficking, and also possession of a gun while dealing drugs.

happened in New Orleans

8

This was exactly the kind of fate Courtney was determined to avoid. From the time he was seven years old, he'd watched as the police arrested his mother again and again for selling drugs. For most of her son's life, Gabriel Miles had been incarcerated, ironically, in St. Gabriel—the Louisiana Correctional Institute for Women. Instead of feeling sorry for himself during the months he lived on his own and the nights he went to bed hungry, Courtney focused on his basketball game. Instead of filling his aloneness with the wrong kind of "family," when guys from street gangs called out to him from their cars, he walked home a different route from school to avoid them. Instead of seeking revenge when friends he loved were gunned down in the alleyways of New Orleans, he walked away from the pointless chain reaction of young black men slaughtering each other. He refused to listen to the siren call of genocide disguised as pride.

Courtney chose another path. He poured his energy into breaking the cycle of unemployment, abuse and neglect that poverty had predestined for him. His primary motivation in keeping his record clean? Setting an example for his Mom so she'll be inspired to finally straighten her life out when she gets out of jail—this time.

Hurricane Katrina was the most destructive natural disaster in the history of the United States. We still honor its victims and heroes today in our music, television specials and series like Treme, books, and movies because, in their forced migration to other parts of the country, they represent an American tradition—the pioneer spirit.

Thousands of New Orleans and the Gulf Coast residents who were left homeless packed their few meager belongings and began new lives in cities far from home. Courtney Miles left, too, but first he took care of the people he loved. Once his neighbors were safe, he traveled thousands of miles to complete his education on the opposite end of the country.

In the words of Euripides, "There is no greater loss than the loss of one's homeland." Over 350,000 people lost their homes on August 29, 2005, but they've carried Louisiana's culture and pride in their hearts, spreading its richness throughout America.

It is my sincere hope for the displaced residents of New Orleans that they will one day be able to return to the city they love and that their Gulf Coast neighbors will also reclaim, in some measure, the way of life they lost the day Hurricane Katrina made landfall. It is my fervent wish for Courtney that he will find the happiness and peace he richly deserves.

Chapter 1 – Prelude to Disaster

Tuesday, August 23, 2005

[handwritten: Hurricane starts in bahamas & florida]

BULLETIN
TROPICAL DEPRESSION TWELVE ADVISORY NUMBER 1
NATIONAL HURRICANE CENTER MIAMI FL 5 PM EDT TUE
AUG 23 2005

...TWELFTH DEPRESSION...OF THE SEASON FORMS OVER
THE BAHAMAS...TROPICAL STORM WARNINGS ISSUED...

AT 5 PM EDT...THE GOVERNMENT OF THE BAHAMAS HAS
ISSUED A TROPICAL STORM WARNING FOR THE CENTRAL
AND NORTHWEST BAHAMAS...A TROPICAL STORM OR
HURRICANE WATCH MAY BE REQUIRED FOR PORTIONS OF
SOUTHERN FLORIDA TONIGHT ...

MAXIMUM SUSTAINED WINDS INDICATED BY
RECONNAISSANCE AIRCRAFT DATA AND SURFACE
OBSERVATIONS ARE NEAR 35 MPH....AND THE DEPRESSION
COULD BECOME A TROPICAL STORM BY WEDNESDAY.

12

Algiers, Louisiana; Tuesday, August 23, 2005 - Courtney Miles focused on the goal. Elbows bent, forearms tensed, he crouched—then sprang, the rubber pebbled ball leaving his fingertips as his 6'4" frame unfolded gracefully. Immobile, he watched it sail toward the rusty rim, teeter, then drop through. The rebound was quick without a net, and he stretched to retrieve it one-armed, then eased back into his pounding dribble on the broken concrete slab. He wiped the sweat from his broad brown brow with his forearm and scanned the empty streets.

Fox Park, his favorite after-school practice spot, was quiet. The suffocating late afternoon humidity had driven most folks indoors in the Fischer Project in Algiers, Louisiana—just "ovah da rivah," the Cajuns said, from New Orleans.

The distance across seemed almost short enough to throw a pair of Mardi Gras beads from one side to the other, but the ferry ride took five minutes.

Courtney's "Wes' Bank" neighbors got by on whatever they could make as dishwashers, cab drivers, and dock hands—most of them riding the bus across the big bridge every day to their jobs. They provided the muscle that powered the infrastructure of the big city.

The rhythmic slap of the ball against pavement echoed through the streets—his heartbeat. Courtney lived for basketball. His coaches said he had talent. In third grade they moved him up to play with the fourth graders. In eighth grade letters arrived inviting him to summer camp. In tenth grade he averaged 11 points a game—on the varsity team. In eleventh it was 17 points. Basketball taught him discipline. He had learned much of what he knew about becoming a man from the coaches in his life, who filled in for his mostly absentee father and part-time step father.

Coach Moore had stopped him in the hall today to remind him about a make-up test in history. Landry High teachers didn't call parents when a boy cut class; they just called Coach. Curtis Moore was a strict taskmaster—from the Bobby Knight school of coaching. He kept a fishing pole wrapped in duct tape that left welts on the legs of players who misbehaved. Each fall his boys laid down bets on when the fishing pole would break, but their prayers went unanswered.

doesn't show up too school

Courtney's first two weeks of senior year had passed quickly. He promised his grandmother that he would work harder to improve his grades—low because of his erratic attendance record. Most days he only showed up at all because he knew Coach Moore would be looking for him. If he was one minute late, he'd catch hell. Coach's practices were grueling, sometimes lasting from three until nine and ten o'clock at night. *all time goes to basketball*

The ball's measured thud preceded Courtney as walked toward home that afternoon, Tuesday, August 23. He moved—on the basketball court and off—with fluid grace, economy of motion, and a sense of purpose. His soft, deliberate way of speaking and his easy pace caused his basketball opponents to underestimate his court speed. The sudden bursts of power he was known for left them slack-jawed with admiration and envy.

There was a kind of authority about him that others saw right away, a confidence that set him apart. His smile was open and friendly in a way that inspired trust, but his eyes were guarded and wary. Like a neighborhood cat that answers to no one, he kept his distance, but there was genuine warmth and humor layered under the feline aloofness. *Milo looks*

The reserve he presented to the world dissipated when he was with his friends. When Reginald, called Slick Puller, told a story, Courtney's sober earnestness sometimes melted into schoolboy giggles. The camaraderie he enjoyed with his basketball teammates, who were like brothers to him, was about to end. They would soon *friends are going to be gone* be separated, scattered across the country, some of them never to see each other again.

Wednesday, August 24, 2005

[handwritten: weather is becoming more dangerous]

BULLETIN
TROPICAL STORM KATRINA ADVISORY NUMBER 4
NATIONAL HURRICANE CENTER MIAMI FL
11 AM EDT WED AUG 24 2005

...DEPRESSION STRENGTHENS INTO TROPICAL STORM KATRINA OVER BAHAMAS...AT 11 AM EDT...A TROPICAL STORM WARNING AND A HURRICANE WATCH HAVE BEEN ISSUED FOR THE SOUTHEAST FLORIDA COAST

KATRINA IS MOVING TOWARD THE NORTH-NORTHWEST NEAR 8 MPH. A GRADUAL TURN TOWARD THE NORTHWES IS EXPECTED TO OCCUR LATER TODAY. THIS MOTION SHOULD BRING THE CENTER THROUGH THE CENTRAL AND NORTHWEST BAHAMAS LATER TODAY AND TONIGHT.

EARLIER REPORTS FROM AN AIR FORCE RESERVE RECONNAISSANCE AIRCRAFT INDICATED MAXIMUM SUSTAINED WINDS HAD INCREASED TO NEAR 40 MPH...

Algiers, Louisiana; Wednesday, August 24, 2005 – Courtney walked home from school alone; he had stayed late to talk with Coach about the upcoming season. Now, as always, he maintained his own brand of Homeland Security—a constant orange level vigilance. His laid-back posture seemed careless, but his peripheral vision was highly developed. He missed nothing.

Courtney saw everything in flat screen; he often knew what was going to happen before it occurred. His coaches praised him for his ability to assess the entire scene ahead of him in a split second and to know instinctively which way to move. He was able to predict what people would do because of his study of human behavior, his understanding of the psychology of basketball, and his ability to read people's eyes. They were skills that made him an excellent point guard and earned him the name Baby Magic but, more importantly, had kept him alive.

In a neighborhood where more people carried guns than drivers' licenses, lapses in attention could be deadly. Courtney witnessed his first murder at age thirteen. The scene still plays out in his head sometimes at night when he tries to fall asleep:

He is walking through the alleyway in the projects on a sunny Saturday thinking through a troubling play from a game the night before. Suddenly, there is movement from the shadows to his left and a man is there. The man steps forward, plants his feet purposefully, and raises his arm. Courtney's brain registers the handgun aimed at him—oh, God—and he freezes, his muscles locked in shock. The breath leaves his lungs. He feels his heart detonate in his chest, a painful mushroom cloud of terror that explodes in his core and spreads icy fire through his limbs. The world goes white and the pressure that shoots through his head leaves him temporarily blinded. He thinks of his grandmother, feels pain for her grief. Strength drains from his body and it's all he can do to stand.

He struggles to focus his blurred vision on the trajectory of the gun and then realizes—sweet Jesus—the pistol is trained on another man walking a few feet in front of him. There is a bang and a flash. A deep red stain spreads on the chest of the man, who has turned to face his attacker, his body in plain view to Courtney—close enough to touch him. The man's face wears a puzzled *look, an expression that is erased when the gunman takes aim at his head and fires again.*

Courtney stares, unable to look away from the ravaged place where the dead man's face has been just seconds before. The blast from the hand gun has torn through the man's head, leaving blood and brain matter on the brick behind him. Courtney's world switches to movie-screen slow motion; he turns away, then is powerless to stop himself from looking back. The ruin of a head is seared into his memory; he will see it for the rest of his life.

Then the shooter realizes there is a witness, a kid—one he knows—who has very nearly stepped, accidentally, into the line of fire. He turns away, hiding his face with his hand.

"Little Courtney, get on out of here," he says. "Move away from here." Courtney runs. The understood code of the street will keep him safe from the shooter. They both know that—even if Courtney recognizes him—he will never tell anyone. He would never put his family in that kind of danger.

This was his first close look at the bloody carnage that plagued his crime-ridden neighborhood, but not his last. Violence was an inert gas that Courtney breathed from infancy. He learned how to fight in the huge brawls that broke out in frequent turf wars. Respect was bought with fists, and with guns - sometimes fired into the air to break up skirmishes that spiraled out of control. An argument at the skating rink or sno-ball stand or on the corner after school could turn deadly without warning, and everyone nearby was pulled in. In a strange twist of irony, it was often the older street dudes who broke it up when the high school kids fought. No one argued with the big homeys.

Courtney stayed safe by following a voice he often heard in his head. Most of the time he thought of it as God, but occasionally it sounded more like his Grandma. "Follow your first mind," was one of her favorite sayings, and he'd learned to trust his instincts - like the time he was supposed to meet his cousin Rob at the skating rink and, just before he turned the corner on Whitney

Avenue to catch a ride there, he turned around and walked back home. When his grandmother asked him why he'd come back, he had no answer, but Rob called a short time later to say that a friend had been shot dead in the skating rink parking lot that night. Another of Miz Geraldine's famous sayings was, "You don't get a second chance at life," but Courtney felt he'd been given one that night. As the massive hurricane gathered strength offshore, he was about to be given another one.

[handwritten: he has good instincts]

[handwritten: hurricane is about to hit]

Thursday, August 25, 2005

[handwritten: increased a lot]

BULLETIN
HURRICANE KATRINA ADVISORY NUMBER 9
NATIONAL HURRICANE CENTER MIAMI FL
5 PM EDT THU AUG 25 2005

...STRENGTHENING HURRICANE KATRINA BEARING DOWN ON THE SOUTHEAST COAST OF FLORIDA...NEW WARNINGS AND WATCHES ISSUED FOR FLORIDA...

AT 5 PM EDT THE CENTER OF HURRICANE KATRINA WAS LOCATED ABOUT 15 MILES EAST-NORTHEAST OF FORT LAUDERDALE FLORIDA AND ABOUT 25 MILES SOUTH-SOUTHEAST OF BOCA RATON FLORIDA.

KATRINA IS MOVING TOWARD THE WEST NEAR 6 MPH...THE CENTER SHOULD MOVE INLAND ALONG SOUTHEAST FLORIDA COAST LATER THIS EVENING.

REPORTS FROM A NOAA RECONNAISSANCE AIRCRAFT AND THE MIAMI NOAA DOPPLER RADAR INDICATE MAXIMUM

18

SUSTAINED WINDS HAVE INCREASED TO 75 MPH...KATRINA IS NOW A CATEGORY ONE HURRICANE ON THE SAFFIR-SIMPSON SCALE.

Algiers, Louisiana; Thursday, August 25, 2005 – Proud of himself for making it to school four days in a row, Courtney crossed the barren, sun-baked dirt yard of the William J. Fischer housing project on his way home. A girl in a thin, tight shirt smiled at him and cocked an eyebrow questioningly. They all knew he'd been with Jamie for two years, but that didn't slow down the neighborhood girls even a little. He nodded in her direction, hitched his heavy backpack higher on his shoulder, and sprinted up the steps to Apartment 2D.

Courtney was born in a Fischer project apartment. His grandmother, Geraldine Miles, helped his mother with his birth on June 16, 1987, and gave him his name, Courtney Mikel Miles. "Miz Gerry," as she was known, took Courtney in each time his mother was arrested for selling drugs—now seven or eight times, he'd lost count. She raised him in the church, supervised his prayers, and guided his manners, but her job as a housekeeper at the Hyatt Regency in New Orleans for most of his life required her to leave home in the darkness before dawn for her early morning shift. When she returned in the late afternoon, she fell into an exhausted sleep, worn out from her hard day's labor. Everyone in "the Fischer" knew that Courtney had practically raised himself. "Streets" as he was nicknamed by his friends, was truly on the streets, left to make his own decisions, unsupervised and alone. For the most part, the people of the Fischer project were his family.

From the older woman who called out from her porch each day if he was late walking to school ("You better *get* on down that road, young man,"), to the men who offered advice when he was

[handwritten note top left: nobody wants Courtney to end up a thug]

[handwritten note top center: everybody looks out for him]

shooting hoops at Fox Park ("try turning your wrist a little more this way,") people kept an eye on Courtney. Because "Streets" was growing up on the streets, he belonged to all of them. Even the police took an interest, telling him, "Don't be like them," if he passed nearby when they were dealing with Algiers' law breakers. And the street guys who were frequently arrested looked out for him too. "You don't want to end up like us," they'd tell him.

Courtney's first tattoo: the word "Fischer" emblazoned across his stomach. His connection to the projects was the center of his being; the "hood" marked his core. He attributed the person he had become to the home that had raised him, the William J. Fischer Housing Development.

[handwritten note right margin: has tattoos of meaningful things]

As a child and all through middle school, Courtney wore the number "15" on his basketball jersey—a number he'd chosen as a child. It represented the 15th Ward, the section of Orleans Parish where he'd been raised. No matter what team he played on, in school and in AAU ball in summers, he played for his home.

[handwritten note right margin: #15 represents where he grew up]

"Hey, Streets, you want a ride?" the street guys he knew often called out to him from their cars, bass music pounding, shiny rims spinning, as he passed on foot. He fought the lure of the lifestyle their drug-centered world could offer him—security, a place to live, money to buy food, and companionship—the sense of belonging he craved.

[handwritten note right margin: really wanted to not be on the streets]

[handwritten note: Where was his grandma?]

It was hardest to walk away during the three months he lived alone in an unoccupied house for part of his junior year. When he felt his resolve weakening, he ducked his head and walked faster. He always tried to get along with everyone, but sometimes when he joked with them, a small inner voice taunted him with the nagging fear that he was looking at his own fate. How did boys from the project ever grew up to be lawyers and bankers and doctors when the only people who spent time with them were drug dealers, addicts, and thieves, he wondered.

[handwritten note right margin: lived alone for 3 months]

He had to make it out of here.

[handwritten note: how was he not caught using the unoccupied house?]

He had to do it for Fischer, for the people who believed in him.

[handwritten: live a good life + get away from the bad]

Friday, August 26, 2005

[handwritten: Category 2 + probably category 3]

BULLETIN
HURRICANE KATRINA ADVISORY NUMBER 14
NATIONAL HURRICANE CENTER MIAMI FL
5 PM EDT FRI AUG 26 2005

KATRINA CONTINUING TO MOVE WEST-SOUTHWESTWARD AWAY FROM THE FLORIDA KEYS...AT 5 PM EDT THE CENTER WAS LOCATED ABOUT 70 MILES...WEST-NORTHWEST OF KEY WEST FLORIDA.

KATRINA IS MOVING TOWARD THE WEST-SOUTHWEST NEAR 8 MPH...

MAXIMUM SUSTAINED WINDS REMAIN NEAR 100 MPH. KATRINA IS A CATEGORY TWO HURRICANE ON THE SAFFIR-SIMPSON SCALE...AND IS FORECAST TO BECOME A CATEGORY THREE MAJOR HURRICANE TODAY AND ON SATURDAY.

[handwritten: Someone afford Miles drugs]

Algiers, Louisiana; Friday, August 26, 2005 – When Courtney saw the business transactions taking place behind the apartments, he knew the weekend had begun. "Hey, Streets, come get you some of this," the man collecting folded bills called to him. Laughter erupted from the group. Everyone in the Fischer knew that Courtney was straight. He stayed away from drugs and rarely drank alcohol. Sports were too important to him, and he'd seen what a life of addiction did to people. *[handwritten: talking about his mom]*

Courtney could smell trouble. He'd learned to avoid it by moving away from it. If something was about to go down, he physically removed himself from the scene. "I *know* what's right here—trouble," he'd tell his friends as he walked away. "I'ma be right over there when y'all get done. I can't be two places at once." *[handwritten: left when trouble happen]*

He credited his clean record to his mother's and grandmother's insistence that he go to church every Sunday. He tried to remember what he'd been taught there in each decision he made. *[handwritten notes in margin]*

Every day he talked to God—out loud—as he went through his morning routine. He chatted about his problems as he brushed his teeth, and he thanked God for looking out for him for another day as he put on his socks and shoes. He was never embarrassed about his faith and, from the time he knelt beside his bed with his mother as a small child, praying had seemed natural to him. He didn't use "thee's" and "thou's" but talked to God like he was talking to Rob or Reginald. The "our heavenly Father" style some people used in church sounded far away to him, so he was more likely to start with "Hey, God, what's up?" It worked for him. *[handwritten: how he prays his morning routine]*

He was about to be "standing in the need of prayer," as his grandmother liked to say.

Saturday, August 27, 2005

BULLETIN
HURRICANE KATRINA ADVISORY NUMBER 19
NATIONAL HURRICANE CENTER MIAMI FL
10 PM CDT SAT AUG 27 2005

[handwritten: New orleans is now a part of the hurricane hit]

...DANGEROUS HURRICANE KATRINA THREATENS THE NORTH CENTRAL GULF COAST ...WARNING ISSUED...

AT 10 PM CDT . . ..A HURRICANE WARNING HAS BEEN ISSUED FOR THE NORTH CENTRAL GULF COAST FROM MORGAN CITY LOUISIANA EASTWARD TO THE ALABAMA/FLORIDA BORDER...INCLUDING THE CITY OF NEW ORLEANS AND LAKE PONTCHARTRAIN. PREPARATIONS TO PROTECT LIFE AND PROPERTY SHOULD BE RUSHED TO COMPLETION.

[handwritten margin: Category 3 almost category 4]

AT 10 PM CDT...THE CENTER OF HURRICANE KATRINA WAS LOCATED BY AN AIR FORCE RECONNAISSANCE PLANE ABOUT 335 MILES SOUTH-SOUTHEAST OF THE MOUTH OF THE MISSISSIPPI RIVER.

KATRINA IS MOVING TOWARD THE WEST-NORTHWEST NEAR 7 MPH. A GRADUAL TURN TO THE NORTHWEST SHOULD BEGIN ON SUNDAY.

MAXIMUM SUSTAINED WINDS REMAIN NEAR 115 MPH WITH HIGHER GUSTS. KATRINA IS A CATEGORY THREE HURRICANE ON THE SAFFIR-SIMPSON SCALE.

STRENGTHENING IS FORECAST DURING THE NEXT 24 HOURS...AND KATRINA COULD BECOME A CATEGORY FOUR HURRICANE ON SUNDAY.

[handwritten: 2 more days]

[handwritten: nicknames for his grandma]

Algiers, Louisiana; Saturday, August 27, 2005 - "Smells good, Grandma Streets," Courtney said as he came in the door and tossed his basketball onto the couch. He sometimes shared his nickname with her, although he mostly called her "Grandmama"— or "Ma" for the role she'd filled for most of his life.

"I hope you're hungry," Miz Geraldine smiled as he reached down to kiss her on the cheek. She always cooked a big meal on weekends, so they had leftovers for the week.

"You know I nevah turn down your cookin'." Courtney's deep musical voice had the wide vowels and spacious syllables of the local Patois. He spoke in soft, buttery tones, dropping the "g's" from his verbs and winding out the ends of sentences slowly like a warm alto sax note.

Courtney washed his hands in the sink, then piled his plate high with fried chicken, collard greens, potatoes, and cornbread. He settled in front of the TV to eat, reaching automatically for the remote control, then putting it back on the coffee table when he saw the clock. Miz Gerry liked to watch the five o'clock news.

"I'm waiting for the weather to come on. I want to see what they're saying about that hurricane," she said as she entered from the kitchen to hand him a tall glass of iced tea. "They were showing all the people on the interstate leaving the city a little while ago."

Courtney shook his head. The evacuation of one and a half million people in the New Orleans area was always a hot mess. With water all around - the Mississippi River, Lake Pontchartrain, Lake Borge, and the Gulf of Mexico—there were very few escape routes. He'd seen contraflow instructions on television—the reversing of all traffic on all inbound interstate lanes to make two outbound ones, but the last time the city had tried it, it failed miserably because people wouldn't follow the "phasing" directions from the governor's office.

Coastal towns were supposed to evacuate 50 hours before landfall, and the city of New Orleans 30 hours before, but city residents panicked and left early, clogging the exit arteries.

"'Lil while ago they showed the sheriff's deputies down in Plaquemine's Parish going door to door," Miz Gerry nodded at the TV, "telling people to leave."

24

"What's the name of this one?" Courtney asked between mouthfuls.

"Katrina. It's still headed more toward Florida and Mississippi, but they say it could turn this way at the last minute. Nagin's telling people to evacuate."

"Everybody always packs up all their stuff and leaves town and then nothing happens." For as long as Courtney could remember, people predicted a Category Five hurricane would turn the bowl-shaped city into a swirling stew of river water and wreckage, but another hurricane in the forecast didn't inspire fear in his heart, or even respect.

Hurricanes wobbled. They hop-scotched. They stalled. They veered off course at the last minute. They zigzagged in another direction.

Courtney had never seen a big hurricane. Many of the adults he knew hadn't seen one either. The oldest residents of the Fischer told stories of riding out Betsy and Camille, but for the younger family members, a giant killer hurricane seemed like the monster under the bed, a lurking presence but one without any real bite.

Courtney had grown up facing down monsters on his own. He had worked hard to conquer fear at a very young age. In the few months his mother was home between jail sentences, she left him alone while she stayed out late with friends. As a small child by himself in their duplex a few streets from his grandmother's project apartment, he cowered, terrified, in his bed. Many nights he pulled the covers over his head and waited, shivering, for daylight to come.

Later, when his mom was locked up and he lived with his grandmother, he was no longer alone at night, but there was no one at home each morning to make sure he got to school. Often he didn't. His many absences at school had led to another fear that he was still fighting to control—the fear of failure.

He told himself things would get better, but his mother never stayed home for more than a few months before going back to jail. Gabe's pattern: home for six months, then gone for a year and three. With a mother who'd been in jail for most of his childhood, his entire life had felt like a hurricane.

[handwritten: compared a hurricane to the childhood he had with his mother]

Sunday, August 28, 2005 – 7:00 a.m.

[handwritten: 1 more day]

BULLETIN
HURRICANE KATRINA SPECIAL ADVISORY NUMBER 22
NATIONAL HURRICANE CENTER MIAMI FL
7 AM CDT SUN AUG 28 2005

[handwritten: Category 5, really dangerous]

... KATRINA...NOW A POTENTIALLY CATASTROPHIC CATEGORY FIVE HURRICANE...HEADED FOR THE NORTHERN GULF COAST ...

A HURRICANE WARNING IS IN EFFECT FOR THE NORTH CENTRAL GULF COAST FROM MORGAN CITY LOUISIANA EAST TO THE ALABAMA /FLORIDA BORDER INCLUDING NEW ORLEANS AND LAKE PONTCHARTRAIN.

AT 7 AM CDT...THE CENTER OF HURRICANE KATRINA WAS LOCATED ABOUT 250 MILES SOUTH-SOUTHEAST OF THE MOUTH OF THE MISSISSIPPI RIVER.

MAXIMUM SUSTAINED WINDS ARE NEAR 160 MPH. KATRINA IS A POTENTIALLY CATASTROPHIC CATEGORY FIVE HURRICANE ON THE SAFFIR-SIMPSON SCALE.

Algiers, Louisiana, Sunday morning, August 28, 2005 - "Did your mom really say she wanted to leave town?" Courtney asked his girlfriend on the phone. Jamie Carter sounded worried.

"She just said she was thinking about trying to find a way out. I guess she's a little nervous about the storm. "

"We ain't nevah left before."

"Yeah, but this time Nagin says it's a mandatory evacuation." Jamie, always calm, was a little tense.

"What's he mean 'mandatory'? Is he gonna come throw people outa their houses?"

"I don't know, Courtney. I just know they're saying it's the first time it's ever happened in the history of New Orleans; they say people need to leave."

"Then Nagin oughta be sending buses and finding hotels for people to stay in. Did he say anything about that?"

"He didn't say anything about that."

"Uh, huh, that's what I figured. So how we supposed to leave?"

"I don't know. The Superdome's open for people who can't leave. They said to bring food for five days."

"At the end of the month? People don't have food for five days at the end of a paycheck. And they for sure don't have money for taking a little road trip just 'cause the mayor 'orders' them to. He might as well 'order' us to take a vacation in the Bahamas."

"I know. I don't think we're going anywhere."

"Don't worry, baby," he told her. "This one's going to be like all the rest of the hurricanes. It's just gonna go right on by us and nothing will happen."

Sunday, August 28, 2005 - 10:00 am

URGENT - WEATHER MESSAGE
NATIONAL WEATHER SERVICE NEW ORLEANS LA
1011 AM CDT SUN AUG 28 2005

DEVASTATING DAMAGE EXPECTED...

HURRICANE KATRINA...A MOST POWERFUL HURRICANE WITH UNPRECEDENTED STRENGTH....RIVALING THE INTENSITY OF HURRICANE CAMILLE OF 1969.

MOST OF THE AREA WILL BE UNINHABITABLE FOR WEEKS ...PERHAPS LONGER. AT LEAST ONE HALF OF WELL CONSTRUCTED HOMES WILL HAVE ROOF AND WALL FAILURE. ALL GABLED ROOFS WILL FAIL...LEAVING THOSE HOMES SEVERELY DAMAGED OR DESTROYED.

ALL WOOD FRAMED LOW RISING APARTMENT BUILDINGS WILL BE DESTROYED. CONCRETE BLOCK LOW RISE APARTMENTS WILL SUSTAIN MAJOR DAMAGE.

HIGH RISE OFFICE AND APARTMENT BUILDINGS WILL SWAY DANGEROUSLY...A FEW TO THE POINT OF TOTAL COLLAPSE. ALL WINDOWS WILL BLOW OUT.

AIRBORNE DEBRIS WILL BE WIDESPREAD...AND MAY INCLUDE HEAVY ITEMS SUCH AS HOUSEHOLD APPLIANCES AND EVEN LIGHT VEHICLES. SPORT UTILITY VEHICLES AND LIGHT TRUCKS WILL BE MOVED. THE BLOWN DEBRIS WILL CREATE ADDITIONAL DESTRUCTION. PERSONS ...PETS... AND LIVESTOCK EXPOSED TO THE WINDS WILL FACE CERTAIN DEATH IF STRUCK.

POWER OUTAGES WILL LAST FOR WEEKS...AS MOST POWER POLES WILL BE DOWN AND TRANSFORMERS DESTROYED. WATER SHORTAGES WILL MAKE HUMAN SUFFERING INCREDIBLE BY MODERN STANDARDS.

THE VAST MAJORITY OF NATIVE TREES WILL BE SNAPPED OR UPROOTED. ONLY THE HEARTIEST WILL REMAIN STANDING . . . BUT BE TOTALLY DEFOLIATED. FEW CROPS WILL REMAIN. LIVESTOCK LEFT EXPOSED TO THE WINDS WILL BE KILLED.

ONCE TROPICAL STORM AND HURRICANE FORCE WINDS ONSET...DO NOT VENTURE OUTSIDE!

Algiers, Louisiana, Sunday afternoon, August 28, 2005 – Courtney Miles, who had paid little attention to the news, had no idea how serious the warning had become. "I'm going over to Jamie's house for a little while," he said to his grandmother. "You okay on your own here?"

"You go on. I'm fine." Miz Gerry had seen the latest bulletins, but she also knew that such warnings had been issued many times before when storms turned in another direction and New Orleans escaped again. Without transportation and shelter there didn't seem to be much need for discussion about their options. At that point she planned to stay where she was.

"I'll be back later tonight," Courtney told his grandmother as he left to walk the eight blocks to Jamie's apartment. "See you in a little while."

protecting his
girlfriend's family

realized he
was wrong
about the
hurricane

how soon
does he
get back
to his grandma

Chapter 2 – Riding Out the Storm

He did not see her in a little while. Courtney had plenty of time to consider how wrong he'd been as he huddled with his girlfriend and her family on the floor all night, listening to Hurricane Katrina bearing down outside the Carter's living room. It was Monday, August 29, 2005, 3:00 a.m. and it sounded to him like the modest second floor apartment was about to be ripped apart. The roaring howl of 125 mile-an-hour winds reminded him of a Halloween soundtrack tape he'd had as a child, a tape that seemed fake at the time. Now, it sounded like the fiends of hell had been unleashed on the earth.

"Keep them away from that window," he said to Jamie's mother, his voice raised above the sound of glass breaking somewhere outside. He herded her younger brother and sister further into the corner, placing himself between them and the rattling panes of glass.

"Stay down behind me," he told them.

"God, it's terrible!" Jamie said. "I never heard anything like this!"

30

"Must be about a hundred miles an hour right now," he said, watching trees bend horizontally outside the window as a flash of lightening illuminated the scene. The boom of thunder that followed a split second later shook the thin walls.

"It's been like this for an hour," Jamie said, checking the time on her cell phone. "When's it gonna move on?"

They'd been watching television that night when the power went out. When the winds picked up around midnight, Jamie's mom told him to stay over. He was relieved to pull out the extra blankets for the couch. She didn't allow him to stay often; she thought her daughter was too young to get serious. He had fallen asleep on the floor with the kids, but thunder that shook the walls woke them up around 2:00 a.m.

They waited now for the violent assault to subside, but there was no sign of let-up. Jamie flinched as a sudden burst of hail pounded the roof and clattered against the air conditioning unit outside the window. "You think this building's safe?" she asked, leaning in to his shoulder. "Maybe we should have gone downstairs."

"Don't worry, baby." Courtney pulled her to him. "We'll be fine." But his deep set eyes were serious, his brow lined with worry. He rubbed his forehead.

"You okay?" Jamie asked.

"Just worried about my Grandmama. I was a fool to leave her by herself." The smooth velvet of his Cajun accent, ordinarily soothing as a bayou lullaby, was harsh with frustration and regret. "I shouldn't have stayed here last night."

"I'm sure she's fine, Courtney," Jamie said. She was his rock, but he could tell she was worried too. "She's got lots of people at the Fischer she can ask if she needs help. Somebody will look after her. Everybody loves Miz Gerry."

"That somebody should have been me. What if she's not there? What if she decided to take the bus over the river yesterday after I left? Sundays is when she goes over to visit family."

"She wouldn't have gone into the city with the storm coming."

Courtney grew quiet, his long arms tightening around Jamie as the wind keened louder. Her wide-eyed siblings huddled close to their mother, trying to ignore the eerie shadows splayed on the wall behind them by the flickering candle.

A pressure-washer torrent of rain pounded the window with a force he was sure would shatter it, and wind poured through cracks in the moldings - malevolent tendrils reaching toward them.

Bam! They all jumped as a huge chunk of debris slammed against the outside of the building like a gunshot. Courtney heard a sharp crack as a large branch broke from a tree. He prayed the roof would hold; he'd heard stories of branches hurled like javelins in tornadoes spawned by major hurricanes.

"Here, see if my cell phone's working, and try to call Rob again. Maybe he's talked to Miz Gerry," Jamie said.

"Yeah, maybe she has one grandson she can count on." Courtney flipped open the phone and sighed. No service.

He slumped against the wall and closed his eyes. Exhaustion eventually overtook him, and he and the Carters dozed off and on while the storm continued. He was dimly aware of the squall lessening to a torrent and then a frenzied downpour. Finally, daylight seeped through his lids and he gently slipped Jamie's head from his shoulder, trying not to wake her. He stood and moved to the front door, opening it as quietly as he could. The oppressive heat was a huge hand that shoved him backward as he stepped outside. Hot wind gusts still flung debris through the streets and bowed treetops, but the rain had tapered off to a drizzle.

"Where're you going?" Jamie asked, rousing from sleep.

"Back over to the Fischer. I got to see about my Grandmama."

"Courtney, wait," Jamie said. She caught up with him on the second floor landing and reached up to wrap her arms around him. She pressed her face against the short sleeved jersey he always wore over his baggy to-the-knees basketball shorts.

Jamie worried about him

"What's wrong, babe? I'll be right back," he said.

"I just have this bad feeling—like I'm not going to see you for a long time. I don't want us to get separated."

"I don't want to leave you either, but my grandma is my responsibility."

"You're always taking care of everybody else. Sometimes I need to you to be here for me."

"Come on, Jamie, don't do this right now. I gotta go."

"Just be careful, okay? There might be power lines on the ground, and they could be hard to see with all the trees down." She clung to him, ignoring the rain that whipped around them.

"Don't worry. I'll be fine," he said, kissing her on the forehead. "You go on back in."

Jamie's family, now awake, peered out the front door.

Yards and driveways were flooded and water raced down the street into drainage ditches. Tree limbs and trash covered everything; the neighborhood was littered with wood and paper and plastic and sheet metal and cardboard and pieces of pink insulation.

A large fallen tree blocked the entire street in front of the house. It looked like the worst was over and, despite the debris, their home and neighborhood seemed intact.

Courtney ran down the stairs and stepped lightly over the garbage as he moved toward the street. He climbed across the giant tree, using the larger limbs as steps. He pushed aside branches that slapped at his face. He ducked his head against the drizzling rain and wiped away the sweat that trickled into his eyes. A pressure cooker of moist heat sucked the air from his lungs.

trees are down every where

where they live

Algiers was still, quiet, hushed. It had turned into a ghost town, an empty city covered in debris. The sidewalks— "banquettes," the older locals called them—were greenly carpeted with lush layers of wet, shining leaves. The houses were mud-splattered in a macabre paint-ball style.

a lot of damage

Courtney's fine-tuned peripheral vision registered flashing blue lights in the distance, down at the corner of Cable and Jeremiah. He turned and saw police cars gathered there; they seemed to be surrounding the bank.

He quickly turned in the other direction toward Fischer Housing Project. As he picked up his pace, the destruction of Hurricane Katrina unfolded before him. Windows were shattered, wooden fences dismantled, and metal awnings crumpled accordion-style. Missing tiles left odd patterns in rooftops and siding hung from houses, peeled off like strips of yesterday's newspaper. Even part of a brick retaining wall had collapsed. A huge tree was ripped out of the ground, its gnarled roots waving in the wind like a beached octopus. Massive limbs had gouged large holes in houses. Many of the stately ancient oaks that lined the streets of Algiers had been snapped in two like pencils or tossed into the street like toys.

Each new scene turned up the dial on Courtney's panic. Fear for his grandmother gripped his heart, and his guilt grew exponentially with every step. He had let her down. He should have been there. She depended on him, the man of the house, and he had ignored his responsibility. He was ashamed that he'd left her alone in the storm because he wanted to spend time with his girlfriend. *feel guilty about leaving*

He turned a corner and a heavily damaged house came into view - what was left of it; it had been completely flattened.

His mind flashed an image of his Grandmother's apartment building, reduced to rubble. In his head he heard her voice calling to him from the wreckage. Courtney broke into a run, long legs

[handwritten margin note: Stopped by a cop]

leaping across deep puddles. Just as he cleared a ditch filled with water, he heard a siren behind him. He turned and saw a police cruiser barreling toward him. The lights flashed and Courtney froze.

He groaned. A run-in with a policeman was the last thing he needed. A conversation with NOPD was seldom finished quickly. He and his friends had been picked up several times and held in the backs squad cars for "trespassing," even though no arrest was ever made and they were eventually released. It was the cops' way of keeping them off the street and reminding them of their power over them.

The bank, he thought. They'd had it surrounded. What if someone robbed the bank during the storm and they thought he had something to do with it because he was running?

Please, God, Courtney prayed as he raised his hands slowly to show that he was unarmed. *Just let me get back to Fischer to check on my Grandma. I've gotta know she's okay. And God, I'm gonna need a little help with this policeman. From that look on his face, he ain't too happy.*

The police car pulled up to the curb, and a cop leaned out the window. He was a young guy Courtney didn't remember seeing before.

"Hold on a second there. Just where you headed in such a hurry?"

Courtney kept his hands in the air. "Sir, I'm just trying to get back over to Fischer Project where I stay," he said, panting for breath. He masked his impatience with a polite tone. He'd learned from a very young age there was a right way and a wrong way to talk to policemen, and he didn't want to be detained from his mission.

"You don't have any business out in the street right now." The officer eyed him. "No one needs to be out here 'til our crews get some of this mess cleaned up."

"Sir, I gotta get to where my Grandma lives. She's by herself over at the Fischer, and I need to be sure she's okay."

The cop shook his head, but his tone softened. "I'm sorry, son, but we're only allowing people out this morning who have businesses they need to check on."

"But my Grandma, she *is* my business."

"Where you coming from? Why weren't you at home?"

Courtney's shoulders slumped. "I was over by my girlfriend's house - on Cable."

The officer held up his hand to silence him, while he listened to the dispatcher calling another unit. Courtney waited, muscles tensed.

"It was too late to leave last night when the weather got bad," Courtney said. "Please sir, I gotta go check on my Grandmama."

The policeman focused on Courtney and the two stared at each other for several seconds. Courtney held his breath.

"All right, you go straight there. I mean it, I better not see you out here again," he said as he motioned Courtney on, "or I'm gonna take you in."

Barely nodding his thanks, Courtney sprinted off in the direction of Fischer. As he ran, his mind shifted gears and suddenly, he was ten years old, racing down the same street toward home:

He runs as fast as his small legs can carry him, following two police cars that wheel into the yard of the project, sirens blaring. He hears sirens every day, but this time he knows in his gut they've come for his mother. It's the longest time she's been home — nearly a year. He doesn't really understand why she's hiding, but he heard someone say something about skipping out on her court date. Things have been tense in a way that scares him while they stay, temporarily, with his grandmother. It is her apartment door he now sees blocked by two policemen as he rounds the corner.

"Gabriel Miles, open up. We know you're in there," one of them shouts.

Courtney tries to run up the stairs, but a neighbor man grabs him and holds him. He struggles to break free but keeps quiet, taking his cue from others who are gathering silently to watch.

"You got ten seconds to open this door before we break it down."

And then one cop nods to the other, and Courtney watches him lean his shoulder into the door and slam against it, hard. As the door breaks, the policemen rush in, weapons drawn. Courtney trembles, waiting for the shots that will end his mother's life, praying these men will not hurt her. Finally, they emerge with Gabriel Miles in handcuffs. The small crowd parts to make way, and they lead her to the back seat of one of the patrol cars.

Courtney calls out to her, and she turns to look at him. Her eyes lock on his for a fleeting moment, then she drops her head. He watches them drive away, then slumps to the ground, crying quietly. He is devastated at losing his mother again, embarrassed that everyone has seen, but most of all ashamed - of himself for having to fight back a sense of profound relief. The months of living in limbo are over - months of jumping at every sound, flinching at every unexpected knock, waiting for this moment he somehow knew would come, when they'd show up to take her away. He feels the terrible weight of tension and fear lift, and he feels guilty for thinking it.

Focusing his thoughts on the present, Courtney raced across the pools of water in the street, dodging obstacles left by the storm and praying for the safety of his grandmother and his neighbors. Traffic lights rocked in the wind and water poured from gutters and roof tops. Finally, muscles burning and chest aching, he came in sight of the Fischer projects.

"Thank you, God," Courtney breathed as he sank down on one knee. The apartment buildings were whole and for the most part undamaged. The door to Apartment 2D looked untouched by the storm. Courtney waited to catch his breath, lifting his shirt to help cool off, and then sprinted across Whitney Avenue. His feet slid in the mud, but he kept his footing as he reached the building.

He took the steps two at a time to the second floor, digging in his pocket for his key. He almost dropped it in his hurry as he yelled, "Ma, it's me. Open the door."

There was no answer.

He fumbled with the key, then jammed it in the lock. He turned it and flung the door open.

"Grandmama, you here?" he called. No answer. Courtney ran from room to room calling for her, but Geraldine Miles was not there.

The apartment was empty. And unbearably hot.

Courtney slumped on the couch, dropped his head in his hands, and tried to think. It was good—that she wasn't here. Somebody must have come to pick her up. Maybe she decided to head north with family members and hadn't been able to get in touch with him. Uncle Gus might have come to get her. He was usually the one who looked out for her.

If Courtney knew she was with family, he wouldn't worry. But what if she'd gone into New Orleans and become stranded there? Or had somehow been trapped outside her apartment? She could have become sick and gone out into the storm on her own to find help. Anything could have happened to her. He left her alone, and now she was gone.

If she left with Gus, why didn't she call him? She knew Jamie's cell phone number. Had phone service already gone out when she decided to leave?

A note.

Maybe she'd left him a note. Courtney went back in the kitchen to check the table.

No note.

He looked around the apartment, hoping to find some scrap of information somewhere.

Nothing.

Wouldn't she have left him a note if she decided to leave with family?

By now, the heat was suffocating. Outside he could hear people calling to each other as they began to emerge from the stifling air of their dark apartments onto their porches. Courtney locked the apartment and ran down the steps to find Rob.

"Rob," he shouted in his cousin's face as Robin Wallace opened the door of his apartment. "Do you know where Grandmama went?"

"Streets, where you been? I was looking for you." Rob's thin face was serious.

"I'm looking for Grandma Streets; have you seen her?" Courtney asked again, grabbing Rob's arm.

"No, I ain't seen her but I'm sure she's—" Courtney was off before he could finish.

"Courtney," Rob called after him. "Hold up, I'll go with you— Hey, hold up. She's my grandma too." But Courtney was gone.

He ran through the muddy yard calling out to those who had gathered, "Anybody see Miz Geraldine? I can't find my Grandma."

No one had seen Geraldine Miles.

Courtney ran from door to door until, exhausted and shaken, he rested on a neighbor's porch where a group of Fischer resident had gathered to worry, pray, and plan.

Chapter 3 – The Levees Fail

→ 29th

Later that afternoon Courtney slouched listlessly with Rob, Jabbar Gibson and Terrence Smith on the concrete stairs of the housing project. They watched the neighborhood kids play in the bare yard where patches of brown dry earth had been turned into mud holes by Hurricane Katrina.

The buildings, tired red brick on bottom and peeling wood on top, had survived the storm without much damage, but the truth was "The Fischer" already looked like a hurricane had blown through. The walls were crumbling, windows broken out, roof tiles were missing, and warped, unpainted boards were streaked with rust stains from window units.

Fischer looked bad before

The shell of one upstairs apartment that had burned still sat on top of the apartment below it, open to the weather. The whole complex was dirty, run-down, and dangerously dilapidated.

"Maybe Miz Gerry e-vac-u-ated," Jabbar said, drawing the word out, making fun of the concept none of them had ever had the luxury to experience. Jabbar was smaller than Courtney, wiry and strong. He looked younger but was already twenty years old – cocky and outgoing, his sly smile spreading beneath his thin moustache when he showed off his keen wit.

"Man, don't talk to me about e-vac-u-ate," Rob said, "Ain't nobody gonna evacuate. We got no money. No car. No place to go."

"What you talkin' 'bout? I'm gonna e-vac-u-ate right now, in my li-mo-sine. You know, the one Ray Nagin sent round for me. Y'all want to come?"

"Pff! Nagin, right," Rob snorted.

"The Man 'ordered' us to leave," Jabbar said, "but he forgot to 'order' us some buses."

"Y'all stop messing around," Courtney snapped. "What if my grandma got held up across the river and couldn't get out? If Algiers looks this bad, New Orleans must have got slammed."

"Was she at the hotel?" Terrence, who was called Nas after the rapper, asked.

"Naa, you didn't hear Hyatt let her go?" Rob asked. "Forty years cleaning rooms and lugging other people's dirty laundry and they fired her just like that."

"They got a radio down at Tidy's," Courtney said, standing up. "I'ma go down there and listen for a while." The other boys followed him down to the nearby porch where neighbors sat huddled over a small radio listening to news reports.

Courtney was relieved that the radio announcer sounded calm. He listened quietly to the news reports of the clean-up taking place in uptown New Orleans. People were mopping water and picking up debris. They were happy they'd been spared the devastation that was predicted. According to the radio reports, the city had "sustained minimal damage considering the magnitude of the surge from the Gulf of Mexico and the fact that Hurricane Katrina brought Category 4 winds."

He heard interviews with bars owners reopening their businesses on Bourbon Street, tourists dragging their luggage in front of French Quarter hotels, and restaurant owners cooking big pots of food to keep it from spoiling in the extended power outage that came with storms like this.

"Sounds like New Orleans made out okay," Courtney tried to reassure himself. "Thank God the levees held up over there."

"Sounds like they just got the same kinda water that always backs up in the streets after it rains," Jabbar said with a shrug. "Good thing we're on higher ground. The wind beat us up pretty bad, but we don't have to worry too much about water on this side of the river."

"Have you *seen* the streets lately?" Nas asked. "I walked down to Whitney a little while ago and the water was over the tops of my shoes. I ain't never seen it do that before." Nas was the youngest of the boys—a baby-faced thirteen. He looked up to the older guys, and his voice was anxious.

"Hold up a minute," Courtney said suddenly, leaning toward the radio. "They're saying something about the 17th St. Canal. They're saying the water's coming through!"

"—again, we are getting reports of a major breach in the 17th Street Canal," the reporter's voice was no longer calm. "Large sections of Eastern New Orleans are now under water. Gentilly—The Ninth Ward—If you're just tuning in, there is a major levee failure—'

"Oh, God, all those people gonna drown," a woman nearby wailed.

"Shhh, listen!"

"We understand that there are hundreds of people stranded on rooftops in these areas that have been flooded, calling for help. We believe there are people trapped in attics as water levels rise to ten, twelve, and in some cases fifteen feet—"

42

Courtney sat with his friends, stunned at the news he was hearing. Unbelievable—that the levees on the other side of the river were failing! Huge walls of water were pouring into streets, then yards, then living rooms, then second floor bedrooms as residents climbed desperately into attics, then hacked their way through heavy wooden framework onto rooftops, frantic to save their families from drowning.

The 17th St. Canal. The London Avenue Canal. The Industrial Canal. They collapsed; they caved; they crumbled.

Something had gone terribly wrong, the news reports said, something that could not be stopped. Katrina's landfall at Buras-Triumph at 6:10 a.m. had brought a twenty-one foot wall of water that swallowed up Plaquemines and St. Bernard Parishes, then bore down on the city of New Orleans as its levee system bowed to her power.

The words "breached", "overtopped," and "compromised" sent icy stabs of dread through Courtney as he gathered with his neighbors in the yard of Fischer Housing Projects. He had relatives and friends across the river, and he fought back tears as he listened to the areas that were underwater. Gentilly…the Ninth Ward… Arabi…Chalmette… Bywater… Treme… Lakeview… Midtown… Metairie.

How could the raised riverbanks levees have failed? Courtney had spent much of his childhood playing on the small grassy hills - some natural and some man-made—that ran parallel to the Mississippi River. They were low enough for people to climb over, without even getting much of a running start, for a better view of passing ships, but they'd kept the river from flowing into the land on either side for centuries.

A few of them were built with concrete pilings and metal sheets driven into the soil, like the Dutch dikes in the story of the boy who plugged a leak with his finger, but most were nothing

more than sloping embankments, little mounds of ground
entrusted with the monumental task of directing the course of the
massive river. Trying to tame the river might have been the most
foolish occupation known to man, but New Orleans had been
fooled into thinking it could be done. The below-sea-level city had
succumbed to the "bowl effect" that many people had dreaded for
years as the muddy waters of the Mississippi River and Lake
Pontchartrain flowed downward into the low-lying neighborhoods
between them.

[handwritten margin note: how levels are made]

Courtney listened in shock with his friends as neighborhoods,
parks, churches and homes took on the water that should have
been held back by levees and floodwalls. Poor levee maintenance,
over-dredging of canals, and faulty floodwall design had resulted in
tragedy. It was an unparalleled national disaster caused by years of
sloppy standards, bad judgment, and dangerous complacency. The
federal government had cut funding for wetland protection and
state and local officials had diverted financial resources to other
projects. Anyone could have foreseen the consequences of
overdeveloping wetlands and allowing levees to fall into disrepair,
but no one did anything. Those who truly understood the danger
didn't have the power to stop those who ignored it.

Courtney listened all day, his head in his hands, to the
unfolding chaos that spilled into New Orleans streets with the
muddy water from breaking levees. He and his friends sat in silence
in their small community just across the river from the parishes
that were now submerged in ten and twelve feet of water. Along
with the rest of the nation, he heard news reporters, choking up
with emotion, describe the cries of people stranded on rooftops
who begged for help as darkness fell. Many were left alone to die.

On the radio he heard the fear in the voices of seasoned law
enforcement and government officials who struggled to keep order
as their tenuous hold on authority began to slip away. Even the

mayor seemed panicked about the fate of the lawless city as he begged, in an impassioned radio speech, for more help from state and national sources.

The first levee breach had been reported by the National Weather Service around 9:00 a.m., but it would be many hours before anyone understood the extent of the deluge to come. It was an unprecedented flood that would eventually leave 350,000 houses submerged or destroyed.

It would take days—until Sept. 1—for the lake level to equalize with the flood waters. It would be weeks before the water drained from neighborhoods left to rot in the standing filth.

Katrina's path of destruction widened as the hurricane advanced inland to Slidell and St. Tammany parish, then moved eastward across the Gulf Coast.

With the highest surge in United States history, the storm systematically marched across six hundred miles of coastland, from Grand Isle, Louisiana to Gulf Shores, Alabama. The deadly combination of wind and water leveled nearly everything in its path.

Waveland… Bay St. Louis… Pass Christian. Entire towns were wiped completely off the map. Long Beach… Gulfport… Biloxi… Ocean Springs… Gautier… Pascagoula. In city after city the winds and water of Katrina stripped houses from foundations, reduced neighborhoods to piles of rubble, decimated historical landmarks, and destroyed homes and lifestyles.

The death toll would rise to nearly 2,000, as hundreds of families searched in panic for loved ones who were missing.

Courtney trudged off, disheartened, to his apartment and lay awake in the deep darkness and terrible heat, filled with the certain knowledge that people he knew—people he loved—were dead.

He tossed in his sleep, his dreams filled with images of men, women, and children trapped beneath the flood.

And he woke the next morning to find the water rising in the streets of Algiers. In some areas, it was now knee deep.

"We're gonna wind up just like New Orleans, buried under ten feet of water!" a woman's voice woke him on Tuesday morning, August 30. When he emerged from the apartment, he found a half-hysterical woman he didn't know in a yellow flowered dress shouting to the people gathered in the yard.

"We never have the kind of flooding they have across the river," one old-timer argued. "Why you think they store all them Mardi Gras floats over here on the Wes'Bank? We're on much higher ground than New Orleans. Everybody knows that." The Mardi Gras krewes, "secret" social clubs designed for New Orleans debutantes, kept their "dens" in Algiers warehouses, where the paper mache floats for the parades were designed and constructed. Military units had also stored their gunpowder on the West Bank for years to keep it dry.

"You look out there and tell me what you see," Yellow Dress Woman raised her voice above the others. "The same kinda levees that are s'posed to keep the water out of the city on the *east* side are holding out the river on the *west* side. And the river's swelled all the way up to the top of our levees now. And we got *water* in the streets."

"Yeah," another woman spoke up. "We may be higher but we ain't twelve feet higher and that's how deep the floods are in East New Orleans right now. Same thing could happen to us. That's just some little hills of dirt keeping the river out of my living room, that's all it is."

It was true that the water was rising in the streets. And Courtney still had no idea where his grandmother was.

He sat on the steps to his apartment with his friends for most of Tuesday. The airspace above them had become heavy with helicopters, and he watched the constant flow of traffic that passed overhead. The pilots could clearly see the hundreds of people

east flooding is 12 ft. deep

stranded on the West Bank, but no trucks or buses came to take them to safety. The same government officials who didn't help them evacuate before Katrina had now left them on their own without transportation after the storm. No one had come to take them to find safe shelter and adequate food and water.

Mayor Nagin didn't have an evacuation plan—well, not one that included them. Louisiana governor Kathleen Blanco didn't seem to have an evacuation plan.

But Courtney Miles was about to make one.

government is no help

its wednesday

Chapter 4 – This Time is Different

On Wednesday, August 31, Courtney sat in the late afternoon heat with his friends listening to the continued hum of helicopters criss-crossing overhead, interrupted by occasional blasts from a distant chain saw. It was the third day they'd spent sleeping late in stifling apartments, aimlessly roaming the neighborhood, or languishing on the stoop outside, wishing they could play video games or watch TV. The unexpected vacation from school had at first been a welcome reprieve, but the excitement had quickly worn off with nothing to do and nowhere to go.

Bored, they watched a large rat poking his long snout into the garbage around the dumpster. Food scraps and wrappers scattered by stray dogs had brought the nutria out early. The giant water rats that swam in the canals and ditches of Algiers had been weighed at twenty pounds or more. Their teeth were said to be razor sharp.

Jabbar picked up a rock and zinged it at the rat. It scurried out of sight but was back again in just a few seconds.

*bored
just
sitting
there*

"Just gon' make him mad," Courtney said.

"He's a big' un," Nas said, making a face.

"Naa, I saw one two feet long over by Jamie's house last week."

"Jamie still here?" Nas asked.

"They got a ride out yesterday. Her mama wanted to go stay with family in Texas somewhere."

"You didn't go with 'em?" Nas asked.

"They didn't ask him," Jabbar answered. Even though Courtney was accustomed to being on his own, he'd felt left behind when Jamie told him they were leaving. Jabbar read him pretty well.

"Did ya'll get some of that food Terrell brought from that little store down on Whitney?" Nas asked.

"Yeah, just some cheese and crackers. I didn't want to take the milk and stuff the little kids need," Courtney answered.

"They're saying on the radio people been looting."

"Hell, that ain't looting," Jabbar jumped in. "It's called surviving."

"That's right, we're just trying to survive," Nas echoed. He had a habit of repeating what the older boys said.

"Stuff woulda gone bad anyway," Courtney said.

The boys nodded a greeting to a neighbor man in a white t-shirt who strolled past them drinking a beer and smoking a cigarette. Jabbar turned to watch a girl of twelve sashay by wearing sixteen year old clothes—and wearing them well.

The power outage had driven his neighbors outside to their tiny porches in search of any small breeze. Avoiding the heat and darkness of their apartments, they fanned with pieces of cardboard or newspaper as they waited for the day to cool down. They mopped their faces, swatted at mosquitoes, and they worried. For three days they had watched for trucks and buses, but help had still not come. Courtney watched the water rise in the streets and listened to the ongoing arguments among their neighbors about whether the river would break through the levees.

"You heard what they're saying, Courtney," Nas nodded toward the ankle deep water in the street in front. "You think we're gonna get flooded like New Orleans?"

"I don't know 'bout flooding but I think we got to get out of here. The power won't be coming back on this time." Even though he was only eighteen, Courtney had a way of speaking emphatically.

"What do you mean the power ain't coming back on?" Nas asked. He was accustomed to frequent outages in the projects. A cheer would sound throughout the hallways when electricity was restored after a storm. But since Katrina had passed through, the darkness and oppressive heat had continued for days.

"I don't think the water's coming back on either. Nobody's coming to help us."

"You mean *never*?" Nas looked at him.

"You're crazy, Streets. They *always* get the power back on," Jabbar argued.

"We're almost out of food," Nas said. "Somebody's got to bring us some."

"So far 'bout all they've done is drop them water bottles on the bridge," Jabbar said.

"Half of them broke open," Nas said.

"What'd they expect, dropping them fifty feet onto concrete? Just throwing shit out the helicopter for us to scramble around like we're dogs or something," Jabbar grumbled. He was tired of being stranded and hungry—and a low priority.

The boys stopped talking to watch an argument brewing between two men in the alley. Tempers blazed in the hot August heat. Emotions ran high for Fischer residents who were awake all night in the inky blackness listening to the sounds of gunfire and breaking glass. A mandatory dusk-to-dawn curfew had been established, but the fabric of a society that had never been very stable was now unraveling at an alarming rate.

"What's all that about?" Nas asked as one of the men stormed off, loudly cursing the other.

"Prob'ly nothing," Courtney answered. "Just everybody getting riled up 'cause of this heat."

"Ya'll hear all that noise last night—somebody shooting up the streets?" Nas asked. "My neighbor's sleeping with a baseball bat."

"What's she got anybody'd want to steal?" Jabbar asked.

"Her baby girl—the one that's fifteen."

"You talkin' 'bout Janelle?" Jabbar smiled and licked his lips. "Oh, yeah, last time I saw her she was looking *fine.*"

"That's what her mama's worried about. That curfew ain't done nothing to help. It's getting bad around here."

"No telling how long we're gonna be stuck here," Jabbar added.

"Them toilets is nasty, too," Nas grumbled. "I don't go in there 'less I have to."

Courtney saw the situation growing worse by the day as everyday sanitation issues developed into a health crisis. When toilets festered, people tried to limit their fluid intake to avoid overflowing facilities without means to wash their hands, and they became even more dehydrated. He heard people with chest pains or light-headedness blame the stress of the situation, but he knew they worried about something more serious. People on life-sustaining medications faced the possibility of seizures and diabetic comas. There was no emergency medical service, and it was obvious that hospital and police resources were strained to the breaking point by injuries and lawlessness. Courtney knew they needed to act soon.

"You heard anything about your grandmama?" Nas asked.

"No, I been borrowing cell phones to try to call my uncles, but there ain't no signal."

grandma still not found

"She's prob'ly alright. She most likely went off with Gus," Jabbar said.

"I wish I had a way to go find her." Courtney rubbed his hand over his close cropped hair. "There's got to be a way out of here. Let me think a 'lil minute." From his 6'4", two hundred pound vantage point, looking down on the heads of everyone around him, he called everything and everyone "little," often referring to his friends as "my lil' pahdner" in a John Wayne meets Harry Connick, Jr. voice.

Courtney had always been the answer man – partly because of his towering height and partly because of the other kids' respect for his calm demeanor. He'd had lots of real-life experience in issues like how to keep the school from finding out that you're living on your own and how to keep quiet when you wake up to find a gun pointed in your face.

"I don't get it, "Jabbar said. "They're saying on the radio we should get out the city any way we can, but when you try to walk out, they send you back." They had all heard stories of gun-waving cops who stopped flood victims trying to cross bridges on foot. The police mindset seemed to be that anyone without wheels couldn't get far enough away to keep from causing problems for them. They didn't allow you onto the interstate ramp unless you had the means to keep moving until you found food and shelter.

"All them people flying over 'cross the river, you *know* they saw us down here. How come they ain't done nothing to help us?" Nas asked.

On a street nearby, one of the few dry spots, Courtney's cousin Rob had spray painted, "Come get us." No one had come.

"I heard there's people stealing cars," Jabbar said in an off-hand manner. "We could walk around and see if we can find one we can get started."

hellicopters see but don't help them

"You know how to hotwire a car, Jabbar?" Nas asked.

Jabbar paused and considered his answer. "Who wants to know?"

Courtney shook his head, "I'm straight, man. I ain't stealing no cars." (He would not learn until months later that Jabbar had been arrested for stealing cars just days prior to Katrina.)

"And how's that gonna help the rest of Fisher, anyway? I won't leave here without my people. There's got to be some way to get all these folks out of here." Courtney said as he reached for the water bottle next to him and took three long swallows.

"Like what?" Jabbar asked. "You said you ain't stealing."

"I said I ain't stealing cars. I didn't say nothing about buses."

Jabbar and Nas looked at him in surprise.

"A few cars don't help much, even if we had some. We need a way to carry beaucoup people. What we need is a bus," Courtney said, "a big ole' bus to load up everybody and drive 'em out of here."

"Where we gonna get a bus?" Nas wiped the sweat from his forehead with his sleeve.

"Hey," Courtney suddenly sat up straight. "I know where we *can* get us a bus." He took off his cap and looked at his friends. "You know where them school buses are parked down off of Hendee? We could go get one of them."

"*That's* what I'm talkin' about," Jabbar said with a smile.

"For real? You mean it?" Nas asked.

"We could try," Courtney said.

"You know they don't leave keys in them buses," Jabbar said. "How you gonna get 'em started?"

"And where you gonna take all them people if you figure out a way to start the bus?" Nas asked.

"I dunno," Courtney said. "Somewhere that ain't here."

"And what're you gonna do for gas even if we figure out how to start 'em?" Jabbar asked. "They prob'ly don't keep gas in 'em when they're just sitting around."

"I didn't say I have all the answers," Courtney said, exasperated, "but maybe we can figure something out." He looked out at the water standing in the streets. "I just thought we could go down there and check it out," he said. "Can't hurt to take a look."

"Yeah, you right. What else we got to do?" Nas was already off the stoop and headed across the muddy yard. Courtney stood up and stretched his long limbs before following.

"At least we're doing *something*," he said. "Even if you're on the right track, you can get run over if you just sit there. All I know is, things ain't gettin' any better. You know what I'm sayin'? We can't just keep waitin' and hopin' that help's coming."

Jabbar stood up and followed them. The boys headed off down the street, with Nas running a little ahead of the older two. Whether their mission had any chance at all, Courtney felt they had to make the effort. It was pretty clear that no one else was taking charge. He felt they had little to lose.

He had no idea that by the end of that day, the three of them would be starting life over in separate locations far from their home in Algiers.

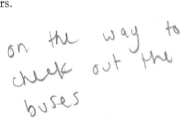

Chapter 5 – The Key to Escape

As they set out through the neighborhood, Courtney felt a strange chill as a bead of sweat trickled down his back. The boys crossed over to walk along the higher ground of the median that ran down the middle of the street like a green garden snake curving through a brown river. They'd always called it the "neutral ground." His grandmother said it went back to the days when the tiny strip of grass down Canal Street was set aside as a safe meeting place for the French Quarter Catholic Creoles on one side and the Protestants on the other to carry out business transactions without violence.

"Water's up on the curb now," Nas worried. "Does it look like it's getting higher?"

"I don't know, but watch where you're stepping," Courtney said as they reached the end of the median and crossed an intersection. The murky water hid potholes from view. It rose just above their ankles in most spots, but slowed them down as they slogged their way to the lot where they'd seen the buses. They avoided the sidewalks—buckled and broken in this part of town.

Courtney tugged at his wet shirt and wished he'd brought his water bottle.

"Aw, *man*, what is *that*?" Nas covered his nose with his hand as a gust of hot air brought a sudden stench that nearly made them gag.

[handwritten margin note: garbage man hasn't come]

"Nobody's picking up garbage," Courtney reminded him. "That stuff's been sitting there since—when was the last pick-up day, Thursday? It's been there a week—rotten food, dirty diapers – just baking in the sun." They were used to Algiers' mugginess, but sodden with the foul odor, the damp air was hard to breathe.

"I don't think it's ever been this hot before, even in Algiers," Nas said.

Courtney adjusted his ball cap to shield his eyes from the sun's glare. "You just got to ignore it, Nas. Mind over matter. When I run track for conditioning, I don't pay attention to the heat. If I think I can't take it no more and I'm gonna have to stop, I just tell myself, 'Kobe never stops. Le Bron never stops. Dirk never stops.' And I keep going."

His friends made fun of him for shooting hoops alone in the heat of the day. Most of them preferred a late afternoon pickup game or a fan-cooled gym, but Courtney used any spare minute and any location available to practice. They accused him of "wasting time," but he knew his dedication would pay off one day if he worked hard to maximize his natural ability. More than anything, he wanted to play in the NBA.

The three boys didn't talk much as they moved through strangely quiet neighborhoods. On a *good* day it paid to be wary in Algiers, and the post-Katrina tension was as thick as the humidity. His grandmother's constant reminder, "Use your senses," ran through Courtney's head, and he scanned the terrain for any sign of trouble.

Suddenly, the sound of gunfire split the quiet air. It came from a few blocks away.

[handwritten margin note: gun shot went off while on the way to the buses]

"You hear that?" Nas asked unnecessarily.

"Somebody shootin' at somebody," Jabbar said matter-of-factly. "I hear they're shootin' at the National Guard."

"What they want to do that for?" Nas asked.

"Cause they're *crazy*. You know people 'round here."

Courtney led the way through vacant lots littered with broken glass and empty cans, across bare yards with bald spots where no grass would grow, around chunks of roofing and vinyl siding scattered by the storm, and over tree limbs that had fallen. Slippery mud sucked at their shoes as they trudged across swampy ground, ducking through hedges and driveways.

They walked past the crumbling building that housed their high school. Once decorated in bright red and blue panels, L. B. Landry's current color scheme was rust and mud.

Even before Katrina its broken-out windows and dilapidated façade advertised its plummeting academic standards.

As they rounded the corner, the bus yard appeared in the distance.

"There it is!" Nas ran ahead of the other boys. "The buses— they're still there."

"Looks like there's about ten or twelve of them," Jabbar said.

The yellow school buses were parked at random angles in the small lot across a multi-puddled yard about fifty feet from the road. Large tires were stacked against what looked like a workshop, and an empty bucket nearby might have been used to wash them.

A black iron fence made of vertical bars about six inches apart surrounded the lot. It was connected by a gray chain-link gate. Even from a distance Courtney could see the chain and padlock that held the gate closed. He noticed the weeds sprouting around the tires of the nearest buses and wondered to himself how recently they'd been driven. Maybe these were buses that needed repairs, buses that weren't running. He'd never paid much attention to this lot before.

"You *know* that gate's locked," Jabbar said as they walked toward it. "I don't see any way to get buses outta there."

"I'm just gonna think good thoughts." Courtney told him. He always made it through the hardest days by believing that things would get better, and they often did.

As they neared the fence, Courtney registered details of his surroundings. There was no sign of activity from the houses nearby, no sound to indicate anyone was in the vicinity. He was deliberating the mechanics of scaling the fence when Nas reached the gate first and pushed against it. The chain held fast. *[handwritten: here is a pad lock on the gate]*

"We could climb over," Jabbar turned to him, "but even if we get one started, we'd have to run it through the fence to get out." He reached for the iron support bars and pushed against them. There was no movement. "It looks pretty strong, Streets. I don't know if we can knock it down without wrecking."

Courtney tugged at the padlock, but it was clamped tight. He pushed the gate as far as it would open, trying to force a wider gap. The slack in the chain allowed an opening of just nine or ten inches. "Nuh-uh. We can't fit through there," he said.

"I can." Nas spoke up, practically dancing at the chance to help. For once, being thirteen and smaller than the older guys would work to his advantage.

"You think so, Nas?" Courtney asked, eyeing the narrow opening. He shrugged. "Give it a try, then."

Nas turned sideways and wedged his shoulders into the small space. He sucked his belly in, making his body as compact as he possibly could, and wiggled his torso into the narrow space in the gate. With one leg on either side of the fence, he seemed for a moment to be stuck, his face a mask of concentration as he held his breath and wedged further into the opening. Then he popped through, expelling a loud gust of air, and turning to grin at them from inside the bus yard.

[handwritten: Nas squeezed through the gate]

"You did it, Nas! You got through!" Courtney beamed back. "Ah'right, now take a look 'round in there and tell us what you see."

"See if you can open any of the doors," Jabbar told him. "There *might* be a bus that has keys," he turned to Courtney, "but I don't think it'll happen."

Courtney squinted up at the late afternoon sun and tried not to get his hopes up while Nas ran to the first bus, pried opened the door, and climbed aboard. Through the bus's window he could see Nas's head bob as he searched under the seat and around the control panel for keys. In just a few seconds, he emerged empty handed, shaking his head. "No keys."

"Just look around back there in that yard, Nas," Courtney said. "Maybe you can find someplace where they keep the keys, like a nail on the wall—something like that."

Nas turned away from them. "Hey, see if that little house is open," Courtney called after him. "They might keep them in there, in that shed."

Nas ran to the white workshop type building and tried to turn the door handle. He looked back at his friends and shook his head. He gave the door a shove with his shoulder, but nothing happened.

"Even if we found keys," Jabbar said, "they're not gonna leave gas in them. It'd be too easy for people to siphon it out them big tanks."

"We can still check the other buses. We only need one of 'em to have keys and gas," Courtney told him.

"Yeah, I guess," Jabbar said, unconvinced.

"Them buses *look* like they have gas to me," Courtney said.

"What're you talking about? A bus can't *look* like it has gas," Jabbar said.

"I'm just trying to make myself feel good, okay? You gotta expect the best and plan for the worst."

They waited in the hot still air while Nas searched the yard. Somewhere nearby a dog started barking. He sounded vicious, and

Courtney hoped he was chained. He had run into the business end of a pit bull named Tonto at age ten when he climbed a fence where the barber shop owner kept his dog on the patio behind his shop. The traumatic encounter left him with a permanent scar on his calf, unpleasant memories of painful rabies shots, and an excessive caution around dogs of all types.

Suddenly Nas's voice came from behind the third bus. "Courtney! Courtney, I found something."

"What is it?" Courtney called to him.

"It's a box. It's on the ground."

"What kind of box?"

"I don't know. A black metal box. "

"Well, bring it out here, Nas."

Courtney tensed as he waited. Nas appeared from behind the bus. "Let me see it," he said impatiently as Nas walked toward them with a small black box in his hands. The thought of anyone leaving a box of keys out in the open yard seemed ridiculous, but nothing was normal about the current situation.

"Open it up, Nas," he said. What's in it?" *found keys*

"These key, these keys," Nas beamed as he held up a plain metal key ring and began waving it in the air. "There's some keys in the box!" he shouted.

"Keys! Yeah, that's what's up!" Courtney yelled. He pounded the gate with his fist in victory. "Thank you, Jesus!" He could hardly believe it. "Hand them out here, Nas."

He closed his hand around the keys, feeling their weight and mass. They were the most beautiful thing he'd seen in months. His heart pounded as he cupped them in his wide palm and counted. There were thirteen keys. Surely one of them would be their passport out of here. *13 keys*

Chapter 6 – Drive

"Where was it?" Courtney asked as he unhooked the keys from the ring.

"Back there behind that wooden chair," Nas said. "It's like somebody left in a hurry and just threw the box down on the ground."

Courtney pulled a small key with a black plastic cover from the jumble in his hand and handed it back to Nas. "Here, 'lil pahdner. See if that little one'll work in that lock on the gate."

Nas fumbled with the padlock and, within seconds, a small click left it open in his hand.

"We're in," Courtney yelled as he pushed open the gate. "Let's go. We gotta see if these keys'll work." He turned and handed half the keys to Jabbar, then sprinted toward the first bus.

"Hey, Streets," Nas said behind him, running to keep up with Courtney's long-legged stride.

"What is it?" Courtney called over his shoulder.

"Do you know how to drive a bus?"

Courtney stopped and turned to look at him.

no driving experience

None of them had ever owned a car, and Nas didn't have to ask if Courtney had a driver's license. He'd had no need of one. Even though Jabbar was a couple of years older, it was a safe bet he didn't have a license either.

"Sure, man. I know how to drive," Courtney said, trying not to think about how little he'd driven - just a few times in his uncle's car.

"But you don't know how to drive a *bus*!" Nas insisted.

Courtney hesitated. He looked at the bus and back at Nas.

"Watch me!" he grinned at his friend and took off running.

Courtney pried open the door of the first bus and climbed the rubber steps. Nas was right behind him. The interior looked fairly clean, but the hot air inside smelled stale. He sat sideways on the springy cushioned seat, then turned and gathered his long legs into the space in front of him.

"Must've been some 'lil short driver," he mumbled as he tried to fold his long frame to fit. He fumbled for the lever on the floor and finally located the metal bar he was looking for. He slid the seat back as far as it would go and locked it into position.

Courtney licked his dry lips. He felt his hands shaking as he reached for the steering wheel and he gripped it to steady them. He glanced at Nas to see if he had noticed. He took a deep breath and surveyed the controls in front of him.

acts tuff but really is scared

"See, it looks just like a car, Nas," Courtney said. "If you can drive a car, you can drive a bus." He hoped he was right.

He searched the control panel.

Speedometer...engine temperature...there it was—the gas gauge.

"Empty," Nas said.

"Now just hold on a minute. You can't tell 'til you crank it."

"Try that one," Nas pointed to one of the keys in his hand.

"What? They all look the same."

"I don't know why. I just think that's the one."

where is jabbar?

"Okay, let's give it a try," Courtney said, inserting the key Nas had pointed out into the ignition. He said a little prayer and tried it.

The key refused to turn.

"Don't worry," he said. "We got other keys." He began inserting the keys in his hand, one by one, into the ignition. None of them started the bus.

no keys went to that bus

Nas's shoulders slumped.

"We got lots more buses," Courtney told him. "We're not giving up now."

He jumped off the first bus and moved toward the second. Then he saw that Jabbar was trying to start that one, so they moved to the third one. The door opened easily, but when Courtney climbed into the seat and looked down, his heart sank.

Manual transmission.

stick shift bus

"You ever drive stick before?" Nas asked.

"Sure, it's no big deal."

A mental image flashed into his head—an image of a car lurching and bucking as his uncle yelled, "What the hell you doin'? Put your foot on the clutch!" Courtney panicked and slammed on the brake. "The clutch, dammit, mash the clutch!" his uncle bellowed.

found a key that worked

I can do this, he told himself now, but the task was starting to look more and more complicated. He sat down, trying to remember how it worked. Left foot on clutch—there it is; right foot on brake. He inserted a key into the ignition and turned it. The bus roared to life.

"We did it! We got it going." Nas yelled, pumping his fist in the air. But Courtney was focused on the gas gauge. It hadn't moved an inch. He waited a few more seconds, then shook his head.

empty tank

"It's not moving," he said to Nas. "It's empty."

"Maybe we can find some gas," Nas said. "Maybe there's a station open somewhere."

63

"Can't pump gas with no power. We just gotta keep trying."
Courtney turned off the bus. "Maybe one of the others has gas."
He jumped all three steps at once to the ground and raced to the
fourth bus. Following him, Nas looked up and let out a whoop at
the sound of an engine nearby. Jabbar had started the second one.

On the fourth bus Courtney eyed the instrument panel.
Automatic transmission. *Thank you, God.* He picked through the
keys and chose one.

No luck; the key wouldn't even fit into the ignition.

The next key he tried slid right in; it was a perfect fit.
Courtney felt his heart pound as he gripped the key and turned it to
the right. The bus responded immediately, rumbling and vibrating
beneath them. He looked down at the gas gauge, focusing all his
willpower on the small red needle.

"Move," he commanded it, his entire body straining upward
as if to lift it telepathically. As the boys watched in unbearable
suspense, barely daring to breathe, the bar began, miraculously, to
rise.

Come on, come on, Courtney silently willed it with every nerve
cell, every muscle, every bone in his body, to keep moving. Neither
of the boys spoke; neither moved as they watched - prayerfully,
reverentially, pleadingly—while the red bar inched upward with
agonizing slowness.

One quarter tank.

How far could they go on that? *Come on, keep going.*

One half tank.

Would that take them to where there was electricity and more
gas?

Three quarters.

It had to be enough to make it out of the city. They could do
it.

Over three quarters.

They held in their celebration, waiting to see where it would stop.

And finally... all the way to the top!

"It's on full! It's on full!" Nas yelled, jumping up and down. "We got us a full tank!"

He was dancing in the aisle, causing the whole bus to shake.

"God is real," Courtney breathed, elated but calm. He knew what he had to do, and now he had the means to do it. He took a deep breath and gripped the steering wheel. Time to roll.

"Let's go!" Nas yelled, running to the back to look out the window for Jabbar. "Look, Jabbar's moving. He must have gas in that one," he yelled above the sound of the engine. The beautiful sound of the engine.

"Quiet down a minute, Nas. I got to think." Courtney gripped the steering wheel of the monster vehicle and then reached for the gear shift. He eased the bus out of Park and into Drive. He took a deep breath and lifted his foot off the brake. The bus rolled forward, straight toward another bus. Courtney pressed the brake again and the bus lurched to a stop, throwing Nas forward.

"Hey, gimme some warning next time," Nas yelled as he braced himself on the wide dashboard.

"These brakes are tight," Courtney said. "I just got to get used to 'em." He looked back over his shoulder. "Nas, watch me back there. We're gonna have to back this thing out."

He found Reverse, pulled the steering wheel all the way around to the right, lifted his foot and eased the bus back in an leftward arc with its nose pointing toward the gate.

"You got it. C'mon back," Nas said from halfway down the aisle where he was watching the back end from the windows. "Okay, stop."

Foot on the brake, Courtney focused all his energy on mastering control of the huge vehicle, pushing back thoughts of his limited experience with driving, mostly on back streets with little traffic. He changed gears and accelerated lightly. The bus moved forward.

Ahead of him, Jabbar was easing out of the narrow gateway. He paused and looked back for Courtney, the same look of joy and concentration on his face. As Jabbar pulled into the street, Courtney pressed the accelerator a little harder and drove toward the open gate. He straightened the bus and guided it through the opening. He swung a tight left onto the road, looking over his shoulder to make sure he'd cleared the gate posts with the length of it.

"I can do this," he thought to himself. "It's just like driving a car—a really big car."

Hands clamped tight on the steering wheel, he nodded stiffly at Jabbar, who had pulled to the side of the road. Jabbar motioned for Courtney to go first.

Courtney was always the leader. From the time he was small, his grandmother told him, "Don't be a follower." The lesson had been reinforced as early as kindergarten when he stuck a large crayon up his nose after a buddy inserted a small one in his own. The painful lubrication necessary to remove it in the emergency room had left him with a strong bias against peer pressure.

Courtney rolled left out of the bus yard onto Hendee Street with Jabbar following close behind. A bead of sweat trickled between his furrowed eyebrows as he drove slowly in the direction of Fischer. "Hey, Nas. Can you get some of those windows open back there?"

"Sure, Streets, I'm on it," Nas ran to the back of the bus. He opened all of the windows that would easily slide down, then returned to Courtney's side.

"Can we get through here with all the tree limbs in the way?" he asked.

"Looks like somebody cleared out a bunch of them. The big ones are pulled off on the side of the road. We're ah'right."

on there way to Fischer

Courtney always said "ah'right" in a reassuring and soothing way, with the emphasis on a long "ah" like a sigh of relief, especially when he needed to be calm.

They turned right on Mardi Gras Boulevard.

"It's still pretty flooded," Nas said.

"Yeah, I wish I could see the street. I don't want nails to get my tires."

"Yeah, we don't need no nails getting our tires," Nas echoed.

"How many people you think this thing'll hold?" he asked Nas, mentally calculating the number of people stranded at the project.

"I dunno," Nas said looking back over his shoulder at the rows of seats. "Maybe seventy? Eighty? What d'you think?"

"I think it's gonna have to hold a whole lot more than that," Courtney said. "We got a lot of people to get outta here."

"With Jabbar's bus, we might can take all of 'em," Nas said.

"Hey, Nas." Courtney smiled, his eyes still on the road. "You know when we were talking about stealing these buses?"

"Yeah?"

"Well, I was just saying it to be saying it. It wasn't like I really thought we were gonna be coming back with some buses."

"I know. Me neither."

They turned left onto Whitney Avenue.

"You sure you want to do this, Streets? You could go to jail, you know."

"I'm not going to jail. I worked my whole life to stay out of trouble. I promised my Grandmamma I was gonna make something of myself and nothing's gonna stop me."

Courtney grew silent as he considered the consequences he could face.

"You thinking 'bout your Grandma, Streets?" Nas asked.

"I'm thinking 'bout not wrecking. Now keep quiet and let me concentrate."

He didn't want to admit how worried he was about his grandmother. He had no idea how he'd find her—but at least now he had a way to begin his search.

Chapter 7 – Loaded

Made it to Fischer

As they neared the barracks style apartment complex of the Fischer, Courtney looked up, still expecting to see the 13-story high rise that the Housing Authority of New Orleans had torn down a few months ago. HANO said smaller units, like the three-story one he lived in now with his grandmother, would foster a neighborhood feel that would combat rising crime and vandalism, but Courtney felt a piece of his past was lost the day he gathered with his friends to watch the building implode, disappearing in a huge cloud of smoke and dust.

As the bus pulled in front, the people on the porches looked up in surprise. Cheering erupted when they realized it was Courtney driving. They were even more shocked when yet another bus pulled in behind him with Jabbar at the wheel.

"Blow the horn!" Nas urged as they pulled up to the curb. He was beginning to enjoy the adventure, now that he'd convinced himself Courtney could drive a school bus without getting them all killed.

The horn brought heads popping out of windows, followed by a stream of people yelling and running for the bus.

"Where'd you get this bus, boy?" A burly guy called Big Red looked down the length of the bus and shook his head.

"Don't ask questions, Red. We got us a way outta here."

"Man, you better know how to drive this thing."

"Hey, Nas," Courtney turned to his friend. "You stay here while I get my stuff. Then I'll wait for you to go get yours."

"Okay, but how come?"

"I don't want to turn the bus off, you know, in case it won't start again." Nas nodded; Courtney ran across the yard.

"Y'all get y'all's things and load on," he told the people who were gathering, wide-eyed, on the curb. "We're gonna drive to where we can find us some food and shelter." Immediately they began to scatter, running toward their homes and calling out to children playing in the yard.

Courtney, sprinting toward his apartment, laughed at the shocked expressions as more of his neighbors came outside. Some were already carrying bags with their belongings to the buses. There wasn't much to carry.

Although their earthly possessions were few, Courtney had never thought of himself as poor. It was a neighborhood rich with laughter and love. Birthday parties, card games, and storytelling filled the spaces left by sparse furnishings in the cramped units of the housing project, and warm family gatherings made up for inadequate space heaters. Music drowned out the sounds of gunfire outside in the urban slum where drug crime had found a foothold despite their efforts to chase it away. These Algerines, as they were called by New Orleanians, were Courtney's role models for resilience, generosity, and a strong work ethic. They were his family.

He watched as they made their way toward the vehicles he'd brought and felt pride that he'd found a way to help them, all of them—the skinny brown boys who rode bikes onto the ferry to cross the river for take-out bags of beignets in the French Quarter, the all-seeing moms who gossiped over boiling pots of red beans and rice (on Mondays, laundry day in the Creole tradition), and the indulgent grandmothers who swatted at giggling children during church. They were a community, a giant tribe that grilled chicken in the yard together on Memorial Day, barbecued ribs on the Fourth of July, and cooled off with sno-balls and cold Barq's root beer during the brutally humid summer months.

In February they always geared up for Carnival season when they would fight good-naturedly for "throws" on Canal Street, the trinkets tossed from floats—beads, stuffed animals, plastic "go-cups," and doubloons—aluminum "coins" with Mardi-Gras designs etched on them. His uncles insulated themselves against the few short weeks of winter with alcoholic spirits sold in grocery stores, drug stores, and convenience stores—a business practice tourists found as surprising as the privilege of walking down Bourbon Street with cups of booze in hand, which kept the party flowing in and out of the bars all night. As Courtney ran toward the stairs to his apartment, the sweet whiskey-breath greeting of one of his younger neighbors indicated a few of them had found their own escape from Katrina's troubles.

He took the stairs two at a time, entered the small apartment, grabbed an empty Wal-Mart bag from the living room couch, and ran to his bedroom. He glanced around the room, thinking about what he would need. He assumed he'd be back in a week or so, and he packed accordingly: gym shorts, a couple of shirts, boxers, undershirts. And, of course, his favorite basketball shoes. They were Jordan's with the name "Jeezy" on them—written with a Sharpie when his friend Jeezy, whose real name was also Courtney, was shot and killed.

He moved aside a couple of the trophies that lined his dresser and picked up his watch and chain. He nodded to Dirk Nowitzki and Paul Pierce who looked down at him from the wall. He considered taking his prom pictures, but they were in the living room, so he left them—a decision he would later regret. After a quick pass through the bathroom to grab his toothbrush, he headed back out to the hallway and nearly ran headlong into his cousin, Robin Wallace, who was coming toward his door.

"Hey, Streets, what's going on outside?" Rob asked.

"I got a way out for us." Courtney nodded toward the window from the open door.

"You driving that bus out there?" Rob had already heard the news.

"Yeah, man. We got to get out on our own. There's nobody coming for us."

"If there was, they'd a been here by now," Rob agreed.

"We got two buses," Courtney told him. "Jabbar's driving one." He smiled at his cousin. "You riding my bus?"

Rob hitched his back pack up on his shoulder and pretended to be considering the question. They loved to mess with each other. Rob had recently been the victim of Courtney's wicked hook shot when he launched a piece of cake in the school lunchroom that landed with perfect precision—on the top of Rob's head. Their friends thought it was hilarious—the splat it made, the surprised look on Rob's face, and the massive food fight it sparked. Rob wasn't quite so amused as he picked icing out of his hair.

"I don't really trust you to drive it, but I trust you more'n I trust Jabbar. Let's go." He nodded toward the stairs and the two raced down them into the yard. People were emptying the Fischer, shouting and running from all directions. Courtney's bus was already crammed with people and there was a line waiting to get on Jabbar's bus. Mothers carried infants, young people helped the elderly, and older siblings dragged smaller brothers and sisters by the hand.

The people carried plastic grocery bags, paper sacks, book bags or pillowcases. Because their few possessions were portable, they were spared, to some degree, the fate of many New Orleans residents who would later pull moldy fragments of their lives from the mildewed mess that was once their furniture.

For many Katrina victims, hours of searching yielded only a few small reminders of the lives they'd lived before the storm.

"Who's that?" Rob nodded toward a third bus that had pulled in behind Jabbar. The driver, a young woman in her early 30's, got out and began motioning people on.

"Don't know. Ain't nevah seen her before," Courtney said in his soft Cajun accent. He shook his head. "She must have seen us take the buses and decided to do it too."

"Y'all got you a little parade," Rob said with a smile.

"That's a good thing. We'll have room for everybody now. We don't wanna leave nobody behind," Courtney said. "Hey, Rob, what about Reginald and them? Do they have a way out?" Reginald Ruffin, one of their closest friends, lived at Christopher Homes, a housing project on the other side of Algiers. Reginald played basketball with them at L.B. Landry.

"Yeah, he's over at the Chris with Quintin and Meatball. I got a text from him a little while ago. His momma's trying to get to his Dad on the other side so they ain't left yet." Courtney knew the elementary school where Reginald's mother worked was closed for the weekend before the hurricane, but he'd heard many city workers were trapped in New Orleans by the frenzied evacuation of thousands when the storm warnings became serious. The roads became completely gridlocked with people fighting to escape hell and high water.

In good months when his grandmother could afford a cell phone, he had always text messaged his friends to save money, and his mad skills in talking with his thumbs were about to come in very handy. For months after Katrina hit, text messages were the only means of communication still in operation. Even though cell phones would not connect calls, text messages got through. Thousands of people who'd never texted in their lives learned to speed type as they frantically searched for friends and family members scattered across the country by the storm. Many left home without knowing where they would wind up, and people were desperate to find their loved ones. Reginald would moan later that he could still hear that recording in his sleep, from hundreds of times of checking for service, "We're sorry. We are experiencing difficulty on the network. Please hang up and try your call again."

The people loading onto the bus were relieved and grateful to have a way out.

"Streets, I knew you'd come through, man," a friend named Tyrone said, slapping Courtney on the back as he boarded. "You *had* to come through." Courtney looked embarrassed as he slid into the driver's seat Nas had just vacated.

"Thank you, man. Thank you. Thank you," came a chorus of voices from those already on the bus.

"I don't know what we'd have done without you."

"I love you for this one, baby," a woman's voice came from the back of the bus.

"I love you too," Courtney smiled and called out.

"Who was that?" Rob asked.

"Got no idea," he answered.

No one asked where they were going. They were only aware of what they were leaving behind—and happy to be together.

Well, not everyone was happy

"I can't believe nobody came for us," complained Kelvin, called Wowo. "Them planes been passing us up, and we're sitting right here. That's messed up."

Someone else agreed, "They know we're here, and nobody's doing a thing about helping us." Courtney and his neighbors had heard the news reports, before radio batteries went dead, of families stranded on rooftops. They'd worried about friends and family members who lived in the New Orleans area. But there was no way for the people on the bus to fully understand the magnitude of the rescue operation taking place just across the river—the frenzied fight against time to save people still trapped on rooftops and in attics.

It was the largest domestic airlift operation in U.S. history, massive in scope and unprecedented in its logistic requirements. Over 33,500 people were rescued from danger or evacuated as medical patients.

The Coast Guard was working tirelessly and heroically, but the people in Algiers felt forgotten, overlooked, ignored.

Courtney listened without comment to the accusations of racial bias. He knew that racial tension in Algiers went all the way back to the days when the city was used as a holding station for slaves brought from Africa for the market in New Orleans. Those who survived the trip were brought to the West Bank to be cleaned up for the auction block across the river.

(Africa may have also been the source of the Algiers' name; supposedly a soldier just returned from fighting Algerians in North Africa claimed the land across from New Orleans looked just like that country, when he saw it from his ship in the Mississippi River.) On the bus Courtney listened to angry complaints around him of a government that failed to provide transportation so those who lived below the poverty level—many of them black—could evacuate.

The residents of Fischer had taken care of themselves and each other before in the absence of evacuation assistance. Many of the old folks had ridden out numerous storms, like Hurricane Betsy in 1965 which brought winds of 105 miles per hour. They didn't evacuate because there was no place to go and no way to get there, but many of them stayed because their deep religious faith persuaded them to trust in God to take care of them. Plus past experience had made them overly optimistic. They stayed because they didn't feel Katrina could be much worse than any of the other hurricanes, and they'd made it through them, hadn't they?

As his friends and neighbors climbed onto the bus, Courtney reached out, welcoming each one individually, his heart racing at what he was about to do.

"Homey, what's up?" he said to Darryl, smiling.

"Maurice, climb on in, son," he said as he shook the hand of his friend.

"Marley, we were waiting just for you," he kidded a latecomer.

"Y'all got to pack in good and tight," he told them as they boarded. "We've gotta get as many people on this bus as we can."

The crowd pressed together, pushing further to the back to make more room.

"Nas, did you see anybody else left on the porches?" Courtney asked his friend, who had just returned with a book sack full of clothes. "I don't want to leave anybody behind."

"I didn't see anybody, but I didn't look around too much."

"Run back in one more time and yell down the halls. Bang on some doors in case somebody's in there sleeping." Nas nodded and took off running. *checking for people left*

The men stood in the aisles and the women and children sat doubled up, every seat filled with three or four people and others in their laps. Courtney made a quick tally in his head and estimated that there were 150-200 people jammed into the bus. He looked back at Jabbar's bus as Nas came running out of the building and saw that it was filling up too. The last of the residents were loading onto the third bus driven by the unknown woman. Courtney was relieved to see his friend Kelvin Hodges boarding the third bus. Kelvin's dad worked at Avondale Shipyard and he and Courtney had grown up together.

"Bless you, baby," a woman named Dinah said as she climbed the bus steps.

"Where're we going?" asked a small boy, holding onto the hand of his mother.

"We're gonna go find us some food, little man," Courtney told him. "We're gonna look for you a Big Mac." The child smiled and looked relieved.

Courtney was hoping no one else would ask that question. He had no idea where they were headed.

He looked back at the crowd and sighed. More than ever, he wished his grandmother were here. He wondered how long it would take him to find her. And how he could live with himself if he didn't.

doesn't know where he is going

Chapter 8 – Roadblock

4th
bus

"Who's that?" Courtney asked as a fourth bus pulled up behind the third. It looked like they'd started quite a trend. As he squinted to try to make out the face of the driver, the bus backed up, picked up speed to jump the curb, and drove up onto the yard.

"Oh, man, that guy's gonna get stuck," Courtney said. "What's he tryin' to do?"

"I guess make it easier for people to load, I don't know," said someone behind him. They watched as the crowd loading onto the third bus split, some heading for the new addition to the convoy.

"Tell him not to—" Courtney leaned out the door of his bus and yelled back at Jabbar. "Tell him not to do that. He's gonna get stuck."

Before he could finish his warning, they heard the sound of got spinning tires. The fourth bus was mired in deep mud. The people moving toward it groaned and turned back to the other bus. stuck

"Saw that one comin'," he said to Nas.

When the last of the people in the yard had loaded onto his bus and the other two, he closed the door.

"We all set?" Courtney asked, looking back at the tightly packed aisle.

78

"Where we headed, Streets?" Nas asked.

"I don't know, Nas," he said as he eased the bus into gear, "but everything's gonna be ah'right."

Courtney pulled away from the apartments. He turned down Whitney and headed toward the West Bank Expressway. With Jabbar behind him, he drove through the deserted streets. "This just ain't right, driving down the street with no traffic," he told Nas.

Levels of confidence in their driver varied among Courtney's passengers. "This is a power move here. You're 'bout to be legendary," his friend Brent was at his elbow, clapping him on the back, while he heard Rob behind him say, "Son, just don't wreck, son."

He drove past Julien's, the store where he got breakfast nearly every morning from the time he was a kid. It had been there forever, but it was known as the new store because the store nearby had been there even longer.

Courtney crossed himself as he passed Fischer Community Church, where he played basketball on the church team. His mother was adamant about two things, church attendance and good grades. He smiled when he remembered all the times he squirmed and wiggled in a pew during the long services at St. Stephen's, where he grew up, and learned to sing "This little light of mine, I'm gonna let it shine." Maybe driving by the church at the beginning of this mission was a good omen, he thought. He always crossed himself any time he passed a church, and doing it now gave him a surge of energy. He usually felt better after praying, and right now he needed some help.

Hey God, I just wanna thank you for this bus and fuh real, thanks for them keys we found. Please help me find a place where these people can be comfortable, someplace where they can get cleaned up and have some 'lil food and some water and somewhere to sleep. They're good people, God; you know 'em. And I'm asking you to take care of my Grandmama, wherever she is right now and help me to find her. Please, God, just stay with us tonight and help me do a good job of driving this bus.

"You can just keep right on driving past here," a boy spoke up as they rolled past William J. Fischer Elementary School. The people around him laughed.

Courtney looked over at the building that held so many memories for him. Not all of them were good ones.

He remembered the father/son breakfast he went to in second grade with his stepfather, Michael Tollette. Courtney had been diving into his plate when Michael's cell phone suddenly rang and he stood up and moved away to talk. He came back looking worried.

"Come on, Courtney, we've got to go." He grabbed him roughly by the arm.

"But I'm not finished," Courtney said, eyeing his half-eaten pork links and grits.

"Something's come up. I'll get you some food later."

Outside Michael hurried him into the car and drove to his grandmother's apartment at breakneck speed. He sat sulking on his grandmother's bed while Michael and Miz Gerry talked quietly in the living room. No one would tell him what was going on and besides, he was hungry.

Finally, his grandmother came in and sat down beside him. "Courtney, your mama's not going to be around for awhile."

His stomach lurched at the news. He felt an emptiness no breakfast could fill.

"How come? Where is she?" he asked.

"She's got some business she needs to take care of. But don't worry. You're going to stay with me."

"But how long will she be gone?"

"She won't be back for a while, Courtney. I need you to be brave. Can you do that?"

He hung his head and nodded through his tears.

"Can you show me how grown up you are?"

That day began an endless cycle of his mother's exits from his life each time she was arrested. Courtney refused to believe she was addicted to drugs; instead, he believed she was addicted to the money she made selling cocaine, and to the material possessions it allowed her to buy, both for herself and for him. After her first arrest her criminal record kept her from finding a job. There were only brief periods of employment, a few weeks at a time, at Landry's Seafood in the kitchen and at McFrugal's discount store (later called Big Lots), and then she returned to the only way she knew to provide for her son. She seemed to have given up on herself.

Each time she came home, he begged her to stop. He didn't want new clothes and nice basketball shoes, but she seemed to think *things* would compensate for the stability she hadn't been able to give him. On his thirteenth birthday she decided to make up for the birthdays she didn't spend with him by throwing him a huge party - complete with a DJ, a dunking booth, a space walk, two water slides, a dance contest, and his uncles boiling crawfish and crabs to go with ribs and jambalaya she made.

It was a magical day—a day to remember forever. "She really did her thing this time," he said to Rob as they stretched across the grass in the growing darkness that evening, stuffed and satisfied. "That was the biggest splash in Fischer project history." But a part of him knew that the memory would always be tainted by the knowledge of where the money came from.

He realized later it was his mother's drug money, ironically, that kept him healthy. She always made sure he went for regular doctor's visits and had plenty to eat. Several of his friends suffered from chronic health problems and numerous broken bones. Milk and fruits were expensive, and orange drink was cheaper than

memories of his mom

orange juice. For many families he knew, starches like red beans and rice filled most of the plate every night.

It killed him to know every time his mother came home that she wouldn't be with him long. It was never more than a few months before she was arrested again. He dreaded the knock at the door that often came at the first of the year, although he never consciously connected the timing of the arrests with the Christmas presents she bought for him.

"Seems like every time Gabriel puts Christmas lights in the windows, you know it won't be long before she's gone again," his grandmother said.

He had come to dread the holiday, both for the vague feeling that his time with her was growing short and because of a terrifying Christmas Eve he'd experienced as a young child. He was seven years old at the time, but the memory bleeds into his consciousness, as vivid as a fresh knife wound.

"Courtney, you have to go to sleep now, or Santa won't come," Gabriel tucks the covers around her son and kisses him on the forehead. "Night, baby. Sweet dreams. When you wake up, you'll have lots of surprises!" Courtney feels a delicious shiver of anticipation, but he turns over in bed, closes his eyes tight, and finally falls asleep.

In the early morning hours a sudden loud BANG wakes him—the sound of his bedroom door slamming open against the wall. A huge hand grips his shoulder, pinning him against the pillow, and he opens his eyes to find a horrific nightmare-come-to-life—a giant menacing stranger looming over him in the dark.

"Don't hurt my baby!" His mother is there, screaming, crying. "Don't do my baby nothin'!"

He feels the cold steel nose of a pistol against the side of his head and he lies trembling, afraid to move, afraid to blink, afraid to breathe.

"Please, please, I'll do anything you want. Just don't hurt my baby! Oh, please, don't hurt my baby! I'm begging you, please!"

82

doesn't shoot him (handwritten)

His bones turn to ice and a roaring fills his head. Time stops. They are frozen in a grisly tableau, waiting for the unthinkable moment when the man will pull the trigger. Finally—the intruder shoves him, pushes his mother out of the way, and runs from the room.

"Oh, baby. Oh, God, I'm so sorry," Gabriel gathers him in her arms and rocks him back and forth, both of them crying. "Everything's gonna be okay. I won't let anything happen to you. I'm so sorry." She lies down beside him and holds him as he shivers uncontrollably until the sun comes up.

It will be months before Courtney can sleep alone again. He waits each night for the gunman he knows will come for him, the stranger who knows where he lives and sees when he's there alone. His mother tells him the man was a thief who broke into the house, a thief who won't come back now, but in his heart, he is sure she knows the man with the gun. The stranger left because he'd made his point; his mother knows the consequence if she disappoints her business associates again.

Although he believes she knows the man's identity, he never asks her. If confronted, she will usually tell him the truth, and he isn't sure he wants to know. Gabriel has never lied to her son—except when she promises him every time she comes home from jail that she'll never leave him again.

Cop cars blocking their way out (handwritten) Courtney's memories were cut short when he turned the corner onto the service road to the West Bank Expressway. He saw a sight that stopped his breath. A cold panic slammed into his chest, sending electric currents down his arms and into his fingertips as he gripped the wheel of the bus.

There, ahead of him, guarding the entrance ramp to 90 West, their avenue out of the city, were two police cars. The cars were parked sideways across the lanes of traffic, facing each other, with only a foot or so of space between them. The entrance to the Expressway was completely blocked!

Courtney's foot hit the brake and the people standing near the front lurched forward. The sudden jolt drew their attention to the scene ahead of them, and they grew quiet.

The swirling blue lights splashed the faces of the two uniformed men standing just to the right of the cars. The policemen were talking to each other and hadn't yet noticed the bus heading toward them.

A couple of people groaned.

"Oh, Lordy, we're in trouble now," he heard a woman's voice behind him.

"What're we gonna do? They're not gonna let us pass," said a man near her.

"They can't close the West Bank Expressway," Big Red shouted. "It's the only way out."

Had they loaded all these people only to be stopped from leaving Algiers? Would they be forced to turn around and go back into a city without food and water, without electricity and plumbing, without doctors and hospitals? The West Bank Expressway was the only road away from New Orleans that wasn't blocked by water, and now it was closed.

Courtney felt his plan unraveling, like the way his life came apart when his mom was locked up for the seventh and the eighth time. He'd learned long ago to hide his disappointment if promises weren't kept, if plans were ruined and holidays neglected. But this was a task too important for him to give up now. Who would step in if he failed? No one had come to help them. He believed with all his heart that no one would. It was up to him to do something. He slowed the bus and tried to think.

He had only seconds to make a decision. His brain raced through his options as the bus rolled forward. If they stopped him, they would surely ask for his driver's license. Even if he begged them to let the bus leave, for the sake of the women and children on board, they were not going to let him drive away with no license. If he kept going and they were forced to chase him down, things might go worse for him. He knew that anyone who ran from the

84

police got an even stiffer penalty when they were caught—and this wasn't exactly the perfect getaway car.

As one of the policemen looked up and then stepped toward the approaching bus, Courtney jerked the steering wheel to the right. He veered out of the left lane, aborting at the last minute his plan to enter the ramp onto the interstate. He swerved sharply into the right lane of the service road to bypass the policeman on foot, who was waving him over to stop. The crowd on the bus grew silent as the travelers became aware of the situation. They waited for the outcome of the unfolding drama.

Courtney set his jaw, increased his pressure on the accelerator, and looked straight ahead. The bus picked up speed as it moved past the roadblock, an obstacle he resolutely refused to acknowledge.

He looked in the rear view mirror. The policeman was standing in the street watching them as they drove away. Courtney leaned forward, ropey veins outlining his arms as he gripped the steering wheel, his body tense and his mind racing. His ragged breathing was punctuated by the hammering of his heart which felt as if it had migrated to his throat.

He wanted to do the right thing, but his instincts told him that the right thing was to keep going. He'd always relied on what he felt, rather than what he thought. He felt, more than ever, that he should keep going.

"I think you should stop," Dinah said.

"Go," Tyrone said.

"What?" Courtney glanced over at him.

"Just go."

"Go, go, go," someone near the driver's seat began to whisper. Several others took up the quiet chant.

"Go, go, go," the compelling rhythm matched his heartbeat as Courtney leaned forward in his seat, his neck muscles tight, his face grim. "Go, go, go." His stomach knotted and his left wrist, the one

[handwritten margin note: turned right instead of dealing with the cops]

he'd always had trouble with, ached from gripping the wheel. "Go, *Kept going*
go, go." He pressed the accelerator all the way to the floor as the heavy bus, loaded to the ceiling, struggled to pick up speed. "Go, go, go," his heart drummed steadily.

The policeman had moved toward his car, and Courtney could no longer see him in the mirror. He prayed for courage as he waited for the blue lights he was sure would appear behind them, the lights that would signal the end of his bus ride and the beginning of his trip to jail for auto theft.

"Is he following us?" someone asked. *Where are the*

"Can't tell yet," came the answer from halfway back. *other buses?*

"He walked over to his car, but he ain't got in it," another voice reported.

Courtney willed the bus forward, barely daring to breathe.

"Doesn't look like he's getting in," called a woman from the back of the bus. "Not yet anyway."

The passengers waited, those near the window craning their necks.

"He's talking to that other policeman," someone in back called out. The air vibrated with tension as Courtney's passengers waited anxiously. Their safety was at stake. The safety of their children was on the line. If they were forced to return to their homes, no one knew when help would come. They knew that for many in the New Orleans area, help had come too late.

The seconds ticked by as they waited to see what the officer would do.

"He's not coming!" someone shouted jubilantly. "He just walked back over to the other policeman. He walked away from his car."

"They're letting us go!" A charge of emotion passed through the bus, held to an excited undercurrent in the cramped space.

"They're not gonna follow us!"

"Thank you, Jesus!"

"Praise the Lord."

They had passed the first obstacle in their journey. If they could make it past the police roadblock, they had a chance of getting out of Algiers and away from New Orleans.

"What're we gonna do now, Streets?" asked a familiar voice. Courtney looked to his right. His friend, Thomas Wilson, had wiggled his way up near the driver's seat. Courtney was glad to see him. He looked around for Nas and saw he'd been pushed further back in the bus.

"We're gonna keep going till we find another way to get on the Expressway."

"What if they're all blocked?" Tom asked. He was a year or two younger than Courtney and wanted to know that Courtney had a plan.

"Well, we're just gonna hope they're not," Courtney said, "Hey, Thomas, look and see if Jabbar's still back there."

Thomas looked back. "Yeah, he's right behind you. That woman, though, the one behind Jabbar, she pulled her bus over and the cop's talking to her."

"Maybe you should speed up a little in case they change their minds and decide to come after us," someone said.

"We're okay, don't worry," Courtney reassured them, although his heart was still pounding.

As they crossed over Whitney and passed the coffee shop that he visited many Saturday mornings, he began to see people in the distance. Near the corner a large number of Jefferson Parish school buses were parked.

"Why didn't they use those buses to take people out of here?" someone asked the obvious question. No one had an answer.

"Maybe somebody'll figure out how to get them started," Courtney said.

"Bet they don't got no keys," Tom said.

"Bet they don't got no Courtney," Dinah said.

"What're all them people doing in a big pile right there?" Tyrone asked, pointing.

Just past the buses there was a large group of people walking along the service road they were on, heading toward the expressway on foot—about thirty of them, carrying plastic bags and pillowcases with soft bulges of clothing. Several adults carried small children, and Courtney saw an elderly man at the end of the line who was having trouble keeping up even the weary pace the others were setting.

"Where're they going?" someone asked.

"I guess they're trying to get out of here too, same as us," Courtney said.

"It looks like some more people from the project. I know that man right there," a woman from the right side of the bus called out.

"Maybe we can make a 'lil room for some more people." Courtney was slowing the bus as he spoke. He turned into the parking lot where a Walgreen's was under construction and rolled to a stop as the people began running toward the bus.

"What're you doing, Streets?" Tyrone asked.

"We're stopping. We've gotta pick up some more people."

"You're trippin', man. We ain't got room. We're already lapped up."

It was true. There wasn't a single seat that didn't have people sitting in other people's laps, and the aisles were full. The bus was packed deep, deep, deep.

"All I know is, I can't pass them people up. We got to make room for some more."

Several people grumbled complaints, but then someone called out, "Hey, that's some people from my church. We have to pick them up."

"That girl right there's a friend of my cousin," someone else said, and soon the entire crowd was pushing toward the back, making room for more passengers in the front of the bus.

picking more people up

88

Courtney smiled at the good natured grumbling as they piled more children onto laps and pushed tighter against the bus walls and windows. They squirmed and twisted to fit themselves into new patterns that allowed for a tighter interlocking of the jammed bodies on board. The limbs and shoulders woven together in a web of unwashed humanity were rearranged in a new configuration. The tangle of people in the hot bus emphasized the musty smells; even the scrawny boys who hated baths wished for one after three days without water.

"Get in where you fit in," Courtney told the new additions to the journey cheerfully as they looked at the sea of faces peering out at them with varying emotions.

"Praise Jesus," one woman raised her hands as she boarded. "I didn't know how I was gonna walk outta here. You're just an answer to prayer, son, just an answer to prayer."

After the people crowded onto the bus, Courtney realized he would have a difficult time driving. The front section was jammed with people, and he spread his elbows outward to clear a space to steer.

"Y'all got to help me keep some room up here now," he warned, "I need a 'lil space so I can turn the wheel." He pulled back out onto the service road and headed for the next ramp of the highway. He squinted into the distance, searching the road ahead anxiously. No policemen, as far as he could tell.

"Manhattan Boulevard," he called out as he read the next sign. "That's where we got to get on."

He leaned forward in his seat.

As they neared the entrance, he looked around for any sign of trouble.

No police cars.

No barricades.

The ramp was open.

He sighed with relief. He pushed the pedal to the floorboard and prayed that the bus could make it up the steep incline ahead. With its heavy load it slowed to a crawl as he climbed the ramp.

Fifteen miles per hour...ten...five.

The bus lumbered upward.

If they went any slower, Courtney was sure they'd stall out.

And finally they made it. They reached the top. Courtney pulled onto the West Bank Expressway, and cheering erupted around him.

"You did it, Courtney."

made it to the expressway

"Way to go, Streets."

"You really are gonna get us out of here."

They craned their necks, looking backward to see if they were being followed, but the ramp behind them was clear.

Courtney looked around and realized there were no cars on the road. He had Highway 90 all to himself, with the comforting exception of Jabbar behind him. Not only was the Expressway empty but every streetlight, every traffic light, every business sign was out. Courtney reached down to find the knob for the headlights although it wasn't quite dark yet. He had no idea where he was going. All he knew was he would keep going until he found light.

power was out on the expressway

Chapter 9 – To Lafayette

no cars + no people

Courtney locked his elbows to keep the press of people around him from interfering with his driving and aimed the bus straight down the dark highway. In the eerie stillness, with no cars on the road and no lights anywhere, it felt like they were the last survivors on earth. The highway that was always teeming with traffic was deserted; there was no sign of life from the houses and businesses alongside it.

His passengers, who had been talking quietly, became silent at the sobering sight of ruined buildings and demolished homes. It was their first look at the damage Katrina had inflicted on the West Bank communities outside Algiers. Everywhere they turned, businesses were ripped apart and houses broken in half or pulled from their foundations.

"Mama, what's that blue stuff on top of those houses?" Courtney heard a child behind him ask. He looked down to see several men attaching a blue tarp to a damaged rooftop.

The blue tarps would soon blanket the area as victims of the storm struggled to keep the elements out of their homes.

The West Bank residents had escaped the flood waters because they were on higher ground and further inland than New Orleans. But the rains poured into their homes through gaping holes ripped in their roofs by Category 4 winds. The storm sent

looking at the damage

huge trees crashing into houses, dropped heavy billboards into businesses, and snapped road signs and marquees in two.

"Look at that – cars all crushed like they was toys," Rob said.

"Garage turned upside down over there," Tyrone pointed.

Hurricane Katrina left an odd pattern in the quilt of the landscape. One business along the Expressway would be completely destroyed, caved in on itself like a homemade cake that didn't work out—and the building next door would appear unharmed.

Sides were swiped off restaurants and gas stations as if by the giant claw of some wild beast set loose on the sleeping citizens. The soggy innards of dry cleaners and clothing stores spilled into the streets. Glass fronts of convenience stores were shattered, and parking lots were littered with shingles, boards, and tree limbs. Courtney forced himself to keep his eyes on the road as the bus rolled past mile after mile of destruction.

"Tom, see if that radio works. Maybe we can get some news," Courtney said.

Tom reached over and turned the dial. There was static until he punched a button and a radio announcer's voice became sharp and clear.

"—removing bodies from attics where residents climbed in a desperate attempt to escape but were unable to break their way through to the roof before the rising flood waters . . ." Tom reached over and punched another button.

This time it was a woman's voice: "—death toll approaching 900 as many families still search frantically for missing loved ones—" Tom punched again.

"—angry at the delayed response of state and federal government officials that may have contributed to the deaths of hundreds of people waiting on rooftops for rescue vehicles that never came—" Tom reached over and clicked the radio off, glancing down at a small boy.

92

"That's about enough of that," he said. "You tired, Streets?"

"I'm good. Just trying to keep my eyes on the road. It's hard not to look at all the mess."

"Be dark soon. There won't be much to see."

"Yeah, I'm just wondering how many people are gonna be alone tonight with no lights and no water—and no home. I know what it's like to have nowhere to go."

When his grandmother had left Algiers to stay with his uncle in Mississippi for a while, they had had an argument about his unwillingness to go with her.

"Courtney, you can't stay here," Miz Gerry insisted. "I've got somebody taking my apartment while I'm at Gus's. You just need to come on with me. We'll only be in Mississippi for a few months—just 'til I save enough money to live on for a while."

"Reginald said I can stay with him until Mom gets out. If I leave Algiers, I'll lose my ball team, and this 11th grade year's a big deal to college scouts. Some of them been watching me since I was in 8th grade, coach told me. If I'ma get a scholarship, I can't start over in a new town. I'll fall off the radar screen and lose my chance."

"Reginald's mom said it was all right for you to stay?" Miz Gerry knew how strong-willed Courtney could be.

"Sure, Grandmama, it's all set. You know I've always been able to take care of myself. I'm fine on my own."

The night she left for Mississippi he climbed through a window into the duplex he and his mom had rented until a few weeks earlier when Gabriel was arrested again. The power and water had been turned off at the end of the month, but fortunately, no new renters had appeared, so the place was empty. A few pieces of his mom's furniture were still there, so he moved them around and set up camp in the cold, dark house. It was the closest thing he had to a home at the time, even though he was alone with nothing to eat and no way to stay warm.

He settled into a routine in his new/old surroundings. Homework, always a struggle for him, was even more difficult in candlelight. At school he pretended everything was fine. It was easy to shower at the school gym without arousing suspicion. He told his secret to no one. He knew he might be sent to Mississippi, or even worse, to foster care, since his grandmother did not have legal custody of him. He knew stories of kids at school who disappeared into a child welfare system that made it hard for parents to find them again.

Miss Pat, the neighbor, was the only one who figured out that he was living there alone.

One evening she confronted him as he was slipping in through the back door, "Just how do you plan on stayin' here with no way to take a bath or wash your clothes?" she asked him, her hand on her hip. "And what are you gonna do without money for food?"

"I'll get by, Miss Pat. Don't you worry about me. I been washing cars down on Jeremiah for some cash, and I can eat a big lunch at school."

"You take this can of beans. Now don't you argue with me. I got plenty more in the kitchen, and you let me know when you need some food." It was hard for him to accept charity, even from a friend, but hunger trumped pride. Miss Pat tried to look after him for awhile, but she respected his privacy once she knew he could take care of himself. He had to admit he didn't mind too much when she watched out for him to leave for school in the morning, handing him a Capri Sun and scolding him a little if he ran late.

Louisiana winters were fairly mild, but the damp November nights sometimes chilled him to the bone. When he went to bed, he layered on every piece of clothing he owned, drew his hands inside his jacket sleeves, and pulled the hood over his head. On the coldest nights, he watched in the moonlight as his breath hovered above his face before it dissipated.

intruder

The worst was the night he woke to a strange noise outside the window. Groggy, he struggled to process the creaking sound, then sat straight up, horrified. The noise just above his head was the sound of the window screen being pried loose! Someone was trying to break in! He had done such a good job of keeping his secret that the intruder thought the house was empty.

scared him off

Courtney groped blindly in the dim moonlight for a weapon. There were no lights to turn on, and he had nothing he could use to ward off an attack if someone came inside. Shaking, he climbed out of bed and moved around the house, making loud noises he hoped would scare off the would-be trespasser. Thank God it worked.

In the unoccupied house he was sheltered from the rain and wind, but he had never felt so alone in his life. Sometimes at night he created a home in his head, a fantasy of a life with the mother he knew Gabriel could be—the mother he'd seen on her good days, when she was her best self. There was music and laughter instead of shouting, and hitting. He tried to push back that picture. He felt disloyal when he wished his mom could be more like the mothers of some of his friends. His love for her was fierce despite her faults.

grandma back

After several months, he came home from school one afternoon to find Miss Pat sitting on the front porch of the empty house. He knew from her smile that there was news. "Your grandma says come home," she said simply. Courtney hugged her, then sprinted the ten blocks to Apartment 2D, the room where he was born in the apartment his grandmother had returned to. Miz Geraldine was back.

The first thing she did was to cook him a big meal. She was worried that he looked thin. They talked late into the night about their separate lives over the past weeks. Courtney confessed to his grandmother that he was worried about his Mom. It had been a long time since she had contacted either of them, and he was trying not to feel hurt.

"You can't let it bother you, Courtney," his grandmother told him. "Your Mama loves you more than anything. It's just hard for her to hear about all the things she's not here for."

He knew it was true. He heard it in Gabriel's voice on the rare occasions he found a way to speak with her. Every question she asked about his grades, his friends, his basketball games reminded her of all the things she was missing out on in his life.

"Seems like every time we get to be real close and it starts feelin' like we're a real family, she's back in jail," he told his Grandma. He took every opportunity he'd been offered to visit her. It never seemed strange to him, talking to her in the big visitation room at St. Gabriel with all the other families; he'd gone since he was seven. The only photos he had of himself with her were in that room, including one in front of a ragged Christmas tree. But there was very little privacy there, and he always left feeling frustrated and dissatisfied.

loves his mom even after all the bad stuff she did

He loved her and he wanted her to be happy. But he didn't know how to help her.

Courtney was glad his mother was out of the path of the hurricane. He just wished he knew where his grandmother had gone. He picked up a little speed as he became familiar with the bus and more comfortable with his role as driver.

"Got it up to 50, huh?" Tyrone elbowed him. "We're making some big time, now."

"Hey, I ain't takin' chances with all the people I got on here," Courtney said.

"I hear you."

He reached up to wipe a smudge off the windshield and realized he'd been so focused on the road in front of him, he hadn't noticed how much the scenery had dimmed. "Is that clock right, Tom?" he asked.

"Yeah, 9:00."

Courtney checked the rear view mirror. "Jabbar still back there? I don't see him."

Tom looked back, peering across the mass of heads behind him. "I think we mighta lost him. He musta turned off."

"I hope nothing happened to him. I shoulda been watching better."

[handwritten margin note: 2nd bus isn't behind him]

"Jabbar'll figure it out. How we doin' on gas?"

"Pretty good, but there's no way to know how far it'll have to take us. Can't tell how much of the state's been shut down by the storm." Courtney sighed. Hundreds of his friends and neighbors were depending on him, looking to him for direction, and the truth was he had no clue where they were headed.

"We just got to look for somebody that can take in a big group like this. My first thought was maybe churches might help, but none of them'd be open this time of night, even if I knew where they were," he said to Tom. "If New Orleans opened the Super Dome, maybe there's some more places like that."

He tried to concentrate on the road ahead as he sorted through the options that were beginning to make his head ache. He took a deep breath and stretched one arm at a time to unbend his tense muscles, unlocking his elbows and flexing his fingers. These were the kinds of problems that were best turned over to a higher power, he told himself.

"Hey, Tom, do you believe in signs?"

"What kinda signs?"

"Like when you're trying to figure something out, and God sends you a sign. Ever since I was a little kid, when I have a big decision to make, something just jumps out at me, and I know what I'm supposed to do."

Courtney grew quiet and Tom saw his lips move. The idea of divine guidance was not just a spiritual concept to Courtney; it was an everyday reality. He felt his muscles relax, his heart rate decrease, and the tension in his neck begin to ease as he prayed.

prayer

God, I really don't want to tell these people I don't know where we're going. I ain't asking for myself right now. You know me, God; I can sleep anywhere. But I got babies and old ladies and children on this bus, and I got to find some place for them to lay their heads. They can't stay in their homes with no power and no water. Some of these people don't even have homes any more, God. I don't know why that storm tore everything up. We can talk about that later. But I do know we need a lil' sign from you right now, something to let us know you got us in your hands. If you could just help me figure out where to drive this bus, I'd be real grateful.

Courtney straightened his shoulders and leaned back in his seat as the tension left his body. He was only the co-pilot on this bus, he told himself. They'd already had some serious help making it this far against some pretty big odds—odds that started with bus keys and ended, most recently, with police roadblocks. He was sure he'd know what to do soon.

"Where're we headed, Courtney?" someone asked from behind him. Courtney pretended not to hear the question, leaning forward to indicate his deep concentration on the road ahead. If he could stall a little longer, maybe he'd figure out where they were going before he had to own up to his current flight plan status of "your guess is as good as mine."

He squinted at the next road sign, still far ahead, wondering where he was. As it came into view, he read it to himself. Lafayette Street. The next exit was to Lafayette Street.

Lafayette Street, Courtney repeated to himself.

"Hey, I said where're we headed, Courtney?" the same voice asked again.

"We're going to Lafayette," Courtney said with conviction. *(Thank you, God!)*

"What's in Lafayette?" someone else asked.

"Help," Courtney smiled. "There's help for us in Lafayette."

"I hope that help looks like food," Tom said, "I'm starving."

"We got hold of one of them MRE's they passed out to a few of the old people. They weren't too good," Tyrone said. "And they were kinda hard to open."

"I know that's right," Courtney said. He'd been enlisted to help several neighbors who'd been lucky enough to get one of the Meals Ready to Eat.

The idea of breaking a seal to create heat was confusing to people who were exhausted, emotionally distraught, and operating by candlelight. Many were elderly and those without their medication had become weak and disoriented, unable to rise to the challenge.

"I'm just glad they passed out them Arizona teas," Courtney said, "even if they were hot." He was beginning to realize how empty his stomach was. He had eaten very little in the past few days.

"Man, I could go for some seafood right now," Tom said. "Get me a nice, big shrimp po-boy—dressed just right."

"Naa, man, when you're really hungry, best thing in the world is some yak-a-mein," Courtney said. "You dunk that juicy pork in that hot noodle soup with some boiled egg—that'll keep you going. Wish I could drive to The Real Pie Man right now. I'd get me some 'yak-a-meat' and some crawfish bread.

"Oh, man, that crawfish bread," Rob groaned.

"And some file gumbo," Courtney added.

"And crab meat, and barbecue. Ya'll are making me hungry," Tom complained.

"And they got that sweet potato pie, pecan pie...coconut, apple."

"Stop, Streets, you're killing me."

"What I could really use right now is a *cold* drink," Courtney said.

"They're passing some food back there some people brought. Want me to get you some?" Tom asked.

"Naa, I'm ah'right. My head don't hurt too bad—if I try not to think about my Grandma." *headache*

"Is your head hurting, baby?" Dinah asked.

"Yes'm, just a lil' bit, but I'm ah'right." The truth was that now that the initial adrenaline had run its course, Courtney's head ached terribly. He would later experience the same pounding headache any time he traveled this same route—when the memories of his post-Katrina journey ran through his head. The weight of the responsibility he bore and the trauma of the uprooting of his entire life would be with him for years to come.

Suddenly the headlights of the bus outlined a small group of people just ahead in the distance. There were about twenty of them huddled on the side of the road near a Shell station, most sitting and a few standing. Tom cut his eyes over at Courtney, hoping he wouldn't do anything foolish. Without a word, Courtney moved his foot to the brake and began to slow the bus.

"What are you *doing*?" Tom asked. *stopped for more people*

"Picking up these people," Courtney responded stubbornly.

The quiet in the bus was broken by shouts of disbelief as the already loaded vehicle veered toward the group of people who began to wave and run toward it.

"Streets, we don't have room. You're crazy," Tom protested.

"I can't leave them people out there. We gotta help 'em."

"Why are you pulling over?" a man's voice shouted over the angry chorus. "There's no more room on this bus. Can't you see that?" Others joined in.

"You can't keep *stopping*," a woman yelled.

"I can't keep *going*," Courtney corrected her.

"Where we gonna put 'em? Just tell me that," Tyrone said.

"Look at these people," Courtney shouted above the noise of the protests as he pulled closer to the group of stragglers, most of them empty handed. "They're in bad shape. It looks like they lost everything." The crowd settled a bit to listen to him. He had earned their attention. "At least we have enough water to share with them."

"We don't for long if you keep stopping," Big Red told him.

"What do you want me to do, leave these people to get sick with no food or water, maybe even die?" Courtney asked as he rolled to a stop and pulled the lever that opened the door. "Just this one more group. They can stand up here with us. Look, they got a baby. A little tiny baby. I'd be a fool if I didn't stop."

As the group crowded at the door of the bus, pushing to get on board, Courtney saw that many of them were wearing clothes covered with dried mud. They looked as if they had waded in chest deep water—which meant they had come from the Ninth Ward where the flooding had reached the rooftops of houses. These people must have walked for ten miles or more! Feeling like he'd been blessed with an opportunity to help them, he put the bus in park and stood to reach out a hand to an older woman climbing the steps.

"Looks like you had you a nice lil' walk across that bridge.

He decided questions about their place of origin could wait. The people—men, women, and children—looked exhausted.

"Oh, thank God!" one woman said.

"Thank you," said a man.

"Thank you for stopping!" the people said as they climbed the steps. One woman broke into tears.

"Just get in where you fit in," Courtney repeated his earlier welcome as the crowd pressed together to make room for the newcomers. Courtney pulled a child closer behind his seat and tried to shift his body to the left to make more room. He could see as he looked back that people were now pressed against the windows, and parents were shifting children to sit on the seat backs to make room. The vehicle seemed about to burst at the seams and hundreds of pairs of eyes looked back at him, some of them angry at the added load. He reached over and gently nudged a man near the gearshift to remind him not to bump it. As the last of the group squeezed on board, he closed the door and moved the gearshift into Drive. And the bus rolled forward again.

Within just a few feet, another group hailed the vehicle from the side of the road, waving and shouting for help. Courtney's foot automatically hit the brake and the bus began to slow again.

"Courtney, no!" Tom told him quietly. "There's no more room. Look behind you."

Thomas was right, Courtney realized. He was so boxed in at the driver's seat that he could barely steer the bus. Any more travelers would jeopardize the safety of the entire group.

As people on the bus began to cry out in protest, the small band of stragglers ran toward the bus, beating on the windows and calling for help. Their faces fell when they saw how many people were loaded inside and the predicament Courtney was in.

"Don't worry, I'll be back," he called out to the group through the bus windows as he moved past them. "I'll come back for you."

"What're you talking about? You're not coming back." Tom looked at him in amazement. He knew Courtney never said anything he didn't mean.

"Yes, I am. I can't just leave these people here. I'm coming back for them."

"You're crazy." Tom said. "You're not coming back *tonight*?"

"That's just what I'm gonna do."

"Then you're coming back by yourself," Tom told him.

"No, I'm not." Courtney said. He meant that God would be with him, but Thomas shook his head and looked away, thinking he was being included in this crazy plan.

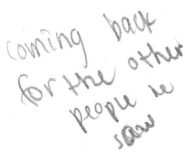

coming back for the other people we saw

Chapter 10 – Ninth Ward Survivors

Courtney's uncle Dietrick had once lived in Lafayette so he'd been there enough times to know it was a straight shot. He drove, his eyes locked on the road ahead. He was distracted by the despair he'd seen in the eyes of his newest passengers.

"We may not be too clean right now," he said in a soft voice to Tom as they drove toward Lafayette, "and some of us are kinda hungry, but we're pretty lucky. You can tell from them people's faces they've seen some bad stuff."

"Where you walkin' from, baby?" Dinah leaned toward a teenage girl and put her hand on her arm.

The girl turned to her with shock-dulled eyes. "Ninth Ward."

"Don't you worry, now. We 're gonna take good care of you. I know you've had a tough time, but everything's gonna be alright."

The girl looked straight ahead, then spoke in a flat monotone. "I saw a dead body. Floatin' face down in the street—all swoll up."

Courtney swallowed hard as he lifted his foot from the accelerator and moved into the right lane to slow down. He was having a hard time concentrating. He adjusted his speed to be safe.

Then a tall man with a deep even voice said softly, "We were listening to people yelling for help from their attic 'till the water got all the way to the roof… and then we didn't hear them anymore."

Courtney's hands clamped down on the steering wheel. His grip tightened.

"I looked over and there were two big 'ole snakes swimming past us," a woman said, "about two feet away. No tellin' what all's in that water."

In the safe darkness of the bus, the people began to open up. They seemed to need to unload the burden of what they'd been through. Courtney squinted into the narrow path lit by headlights and tried to block out the voices behind him. He knew he had to use every bit of his concentration to maneuver the giant vehicle; his lack of driving experience required total focus to do the job.

nasty water

"We was wadin' in water up to our neck," said a young woman holding a toddler. "It was nasty—all full of garbage and sewage. I was tryin' to hold my baby's head up out the water, just prayin' I didn't trip on somethin' I couldn't see."

"You could see gas and oil and chemicals in the water – cleaning fluid and paint remover and pesticides," a man said. "And the smell from rotten food and dead animals, it was terrible." Courtney's new passengers had waded in the toxic gumbo, the rotting roux, the stench that became more unbearable as bloated bodies, urine, feces, and decaying food cooked day after day in the hot August sun.

The bus riders had been force to wade into bizarre baptismal waters filled with water snakes and decomposing human corpses in order to start new lives outside their lost neighborhoods.

"We had to fight with the nutria for dry space on top of the roof," a woman said. "My husband was knocking them off in the water with a piece of wood he pulled off the house. Those big old rats'd just swim right back and climb up there again."

Their stories wove their way in and out of Courtney's consciousness while he struggled to train his attention on his driving. His head began to throb again as he tried not to listen to the low voices behind him.

tried to forget all the stories + damage outside

"My Toby, I could hear him crying out in his pen in the back yard," an elderly man whispered. "He was yelping and barking and I couldn't get to him 'cause the water—it was coming in too fast." A sob escaped him. "Thirteen years he was my best friend and I let him die. He was waiting for me to come save him and I couldn't—I couldn't get to him." He broke off, crying quietly.

Courtney took a deep breath and fought back the lump in his throat. It all seemed like a nightmare. Impossible—that the stories he was hearing had happened, not in some third world country far away, but just a few miles from his home. These people had escaped from flood waters as high as seventeen feet in some areas. Hundreds of people had drowned.

"The kids," one woman said, "the kids've seen things kids shouldn't oughta see. We tried to cover up one of the bodies with some plywood, but the rats..." She trailed off. "Them babies, they'll see that stuff for the rest of their lives."

Courtney had seen the vacant expressions and distant gazes of the children who'd boarded the bus, the horrors they'd witnessed reflected in their eyes.

"They put big X's on the houses so they'd know how many people was dead in there," a woman said. "They didn't want to spend no time goin' back in the ones that already been searched."

"A man on a rescue boat told me they had to just tie down the bodies inside to keep 'em from floatin' away so they could go help the people who were alive," another man said.

"We tried to rest on the ramp up to the interstate, but those policemen they brought in—dressed all in black—made us move," one of the men on the bus said. "There was one that was yelling in my mama's face. He was talking to her like she was a animal or something. They were waving guns in our faces and acting like we done something wrong." Courtney had heard about paramilitary troops who roamed the streets in full battle gear and treated terrified residents like enemy combatants. They had been brought in to supplement the Louisiana National Guard since many of their troops had been deployed to Iraq, and the police force desperately needed help.

rude because they had no answers

Television footage in the months after Katrina would show heavily armed police officers waving guns and shouting at the angry crowds of displaced people who wanted to know about evacuation and water and food and shelter and toilets and transportation, heart medications, kidney dialysis, diabetic treatment, dead bodies, baby formula, diapers. Emotionally drained and exhausted policemen were forced to admit they had no answers. Many seemed to feel the threat of deadly force was their only weapon in the face of anarchy that threatened to erupt at any moment in a city with one of the highest murder rates in the country.

"Some of the cops was takin' stuff from the Wal-Mart store too. I saw one of 'em carrying out a big old TV," a raspy-voiced woman whispered. Courtney had heard stories from neighbors over the last few days about cops who took advantage of the chaos to join in the looting. He'd also heard on the radio news that there were hundreds of dedicated policemen who sent their families on without them and stayed behind to help control the dangerous scene unfolding in New Orleans. He couldn't know at the time that he would face another run-in with law enforcement later that night and the success of his mission would hinge on whether the man who stopped him was one of the "good" guys.

"They told us the po-lice had authority to shoot anyone who got in their way," a man said. "Man, I was just makin' sure I stayed outa their way; they had some big ass guns."

"I know the levees was blown up on purpose," an angry voice said. "Mayor Nagin and all the rest of them blew up the Industrial Canal to save downtown. They did it before—way back in the 20's. Everybody knows it."

"It's true. I heard the explosion, right near my house," agreed a woman. "And then the water came, so fast... so fast we could

Levees blown up on purpose

barely make it up to the attic stairs. It just *kept* coming. We had to
cut a hole in the roof and climb out on top of the house. We were
up there all night 'til a boat came the next day and picked us up. I
ain't never been so scared. I just prayed to Jesus. I never thought
nothing like this could happen. I never thought they'd blow up the
levees 'til I heard that big bang." This was an accusation that would
be repeated over the next few days. News reports blamed the
sound many people heard on a barge that broke through the levee,
but it was true that city leaders had dynamited levees near St.
Bernard parish in 1927, deliberately flooding the farms and homes
of rural people to save downtown New Orleans. Mayor Nagin
called the Katrina rumor ridiculous and said such a feat was not
even possible in the middle of a hurricane, let alone likely. He
pointed out that plenty of wealthy white neighborhoods had also
been destroyed.

Courtney didn't get involved in discussions of racism; he
didn't feel they were productive. He understood the frustration,
however, of poorly performing schools, joblessness, inadequate
health care and substandard housing. He wasn't surprised that
people believed government spending decisions for levee
maintenance had been based on the economic status of each
neighborhood. The Ninth Ward was certainly at the bottom of the
food chain—a low priority for politicians seeking campaign
contributions. He would later see racial divisions further widened
when national news channels called black city residents "looters"
while portraying white hurricane victims as food gatherers.

Stories of rape and murder in the Superdome eventually
proved to be fabrications by reporters playing to racial stereotypes.

Courtney listened to the accusations swirling around him from
people who were angry at the government's inadequate preparation
for the storm and its slow response to help its victims. He was an
American citizen. He had never given much thought to the
government's role—or his own—a crisis situation, but he had

always believed all citizens would be treated humanely. He had grown up believing the leaders of his country would take care of its people in the face of any disaster that might befall them, that this was his birthright. Now he was dealing with the fallout of an ill-prepared emergency management system that revealed shocking flaws at every level of authority from local to state to national. He had never dreamed that his own government's emergency response system could fail so miserably.

"We're all the way to Morgan City. How come there's still no traffic?" someone said. Courtney was not always able to tell who had spoken without taking his eyes off the road, something he tried not to do.

Another voice: "No cars, no lights, no gas, no people. I didn't know it was gonna be like this. Where'd everybody go?"

In the yellow bus rolling through the black night, the passengers felt uneasy on the empty highway. They were all alone in a dark landscape without electricity.

"It's just 'cause they're not letting anybody go this way," Courtney tried to reassure them. "They musta decided not to stop us when we went around the roadblock, but the road's still closed."

"Those cops were probably thinking that's about 200 people we don't have to take care of anymore," a woman spoke up.

"Yeah, it's crazy. You know, on the radio, they're telling people to get out any way you can," Courtney said, "and then they try to stop the people trying to leave."

Courtney, too, would have felt more comfortable if there were other cars on the road, but he smiled to himself at the picture they would make to anyone who came along—a bright yellow bus stuffed to the gills with people, driving down an inky black deserted highway that was lit for miles by only moonlight. And here he was hoping to avoid attracting the attention of the police!

It was strange that he felt isolated now—surrounded by hundreds of people—when he'd been alone for so much of his life.

108

Maybe everyone in charge of a group of people felt this way—the loneliness of being on the front line. He'd been a leader on the basketball court for most of his life, forced to make split-second decisions that had large consequences for the team. In an important game last year he'd given up a three-point opportunity late in the game, bringing down the coach's fury when they lost by three points. He'd trusted a teammate, who had a better shot than he did, he told the coach. "If three men are on me, somebody's open." It had been his decision, and he'd made the wrong one. He walked a fine line between guiding his team and taking too much control.

"Hey, look, there's a car," a boy near the front yelled, pointing.

"Yeah, I see another one," someone else said.

"I'm kind of glad to see them, to tell you the truth." Courtney said.

"They got the power on up here!" someone shouted. It had been days since they'd seen electricity and the yellow glow of street lights was as welcome as the gold at the end of the rainbow that was supposed to come after a storm.

"This one we're coming up on is a sheriff's car," Tom said as they pulled closer to the car ahead of them. "It's one of them Crown Vic's."

"What if he stops us?" someone else asked.

"They're not gonna stop us. Don't worry," Courtney said. "They were *telling* folks to get out the city any way they can."

"I don't think they were saying to steal a school bus," a woman near him said. Courtney turned his head to look at her. "Not that I have anything against stealing school buses," she added quickly.

"Maybe you shouldn't pass him up," a man said. "We could just stay back behind him."

"It'll be okay," Courtney hoped he was right as he eased up even with the car, which was traveling at only about 40 miles an hour.

The uniformed officer driving looked over at them, glanced back at the road, and then looked again in surprise. His double take took in the bus with its passengers crammed into every inch of space, and then he made eye contact with the driver. He slowly smiled and nodded at him. Courtney breathed a sigh of relief, smiled and nodded back, and drove on past him.

"See, we're gonna be *ah'right*," he said again.

"That's another one right there, another po-lice car," someone said.

"Don't worry. He ain't gonna try and stop us either," Courtney said.

As they pulled alongside the second one, the policeman looked over at the bus. They waited for his reaction, which was almost immediate. He gave them grave nod and a "thumbs up" sign.

Courtney hoped this was a sign that he wouldn't be going to jail.

Cops right
drove him
past

Chapter 11 – Promises to Keep

"Hey, Streets," Tom said after a while. "Where you gonna go when we get to Lafayette?"

"I been thinking about that. If they set up some place to help people, it might be at the Cajundome, like they set up the Superdome for people to go to, you know what I'm saying?"

"Yeah, you might be right. Do you know how to get there?"

"Uh-huh, I played there—in the Final Four, my sophomore year." It was a memory Courtney preferred not to resurrect, a disappointing loss for the Landry team.

Tom nodded and the silence settled back in for a time.

"Hey, Streets?"

"Yeah?"

"What you gonna do if there ain't nobody at the Cajundome?"

"I don't know, man," Courtney answered. "All I know is, slow motion is better than no motion."

Courtney knew they were getting close when he saw the turn-off to New Iberia. A little later, as the lights of Lafayette came into view, people began to stir. They were cramped and uncomfortable, but no one had complained. Still, they were ready to get off the impossibly crowded bus.

"There it is," Courtney said, pointing to the sign ahead of them "University of Louisiana at Lafayette. This is where we turn off." He slowed the bus and pulled into the exit lane.

"What do we do now?" Tom asked as they pulled onto Highway 167.

"Just keep a eye out for the dome. It's kinda hard to miss."

"Is that it?" someone asked a little later when a large building appeared up ahead.

"No, that's the Coliseum," Courtney said.

"Hey, look, Cajundome Boulevard," Tom said pointing to a street sign.

"Uh-huh," Courtney said, "See, I told you it was easy to find."

They turned onto Cajundome Boulevard, Courtney praying silently that there would be someone there to help them. He had no idea where they could go if his instincts were wrong.

He drove on, hoping for help, praying for shelter, believing he'd done the right thing.

And then they saw it. *power on +*

Just ahead. *people everywhere*

A huge round roof silhouetted against the night sky.

The Cajundome. The parking lot was full of cars and there were people everywhere.

"Well, I'll be damned," Tyrone said. "Sumbitch lit up like a spaceship!

Courtney felt air escape his lungs, air he wasn't aware he'd been holding in.

"I hope it ain't like stories I heard about the Superdome," a woman said.

"I know one thing. I'm getting *off* this bus," Tyrone said.

Courtney eased the bus into the parking lot. The little knot of worry in his stomach was growing. In spite of the "pass" he'd been given by policemen on the road, he thought about what could happen when their trip ended. He had stolen a bus. He preferred to think of it as "borrowing," but he wasn't sure the authorities in Lafayette would see it that way. It was certainly possible that they'd arrest him when they learned what he had done.

"What's the matter, Streets?" Tom asked him, "You don't look too happy."

"I *am* happy—real happy we found some help. But I can't get too excited when I still don't know where my grandmamma is. And I don't want to get arrested."

"You saw how that cop acted. He didn't have a problem with you driving the bus. I 'magine he knew it wasn't yours."

"Let's hope they feel that way, too." Courtney looked toward the front door of the dome and Tom, following his gaze, saw the National Guard soldiers.

Courtney rubbed his forehead. He had worked so hard to stay out of trouble. Sometimes it felt like everybody he knew had been locked up."

"Hey, Courtney. Maybe they don't have to know who was driving. Pull over there on the curb and let's just keep a low profile for now."

Courtney nodded agreement and, driving slowly past the entrance to the front of the building, he pulled around to the side and eased up to the curb near the street.

There were tables set up out front, and a long line of people snaked from the door to the street. Courtney rolled to a stop, put the bus in Park, and opened the door.

He stepped down onto the pavement with the first group of people to unload, and waited for the tall, official-looking man he'd seen walking toward them. He braced himself for the questions he was sure would come.

"Are y'all from the Superdome?" the man asked an older man near him.

"No, we came from Algiers," Courtney answered, stepping up and speaking with authority as he made eye contact.

"That's not what I'd call a low profile," Tom groaned.

The man nodded at Courtney, then looked up at the crowded windows and the flood of people spilling from the door of the bus. "How many people you *got* on that bus?" he asked.

"Beaucoup people. I'm not fuh'sure. I figure it's over 200."

The man whistled and looked again in astonishment at the sea of faces peering back at him through the glare of the parking lot lights against the windows. An older man stumbled as he stepped from the last step onto the pavement and had to be supported. Many of the people unloading were dazed, dehydrated, and disoriented.

"What do we need to do?" Courtney asked the man.

"Just head over that way and get in line." He pointed.

As the large group began to shuffle wearily toward the line outside the Cajundome, a woman with a Red Cross badge came toward them. The man who'd directed them to the front of the building spoke with her briefly, both of them glancing over frequently at Courtney's passengers.

"All right then, everyone," she raised her voice. "You'll need to line up for your physical examination." She motioned the exhausted travelers in the right direction. "We just need you to answer a few questions before you enter the building."

"Is there someplace we can get cleaned up here?" Dinah asked.

"Yes, we do have showers," the Red Cross lady raised her voice so everyone could hear, "and cots, and food, and water. You'll be well taken care of here."

"Thank you, ma'am. We ain't had no running water for three days," Rhonda said.

They split into smaller groups as they entered the lines that were already formed. Courtney walked around the group toward the front of the line to check it out. He wanted to know what they could expect. And he wanted to look for his Grandmother.

"Any coughs? Diarrhea?" he heard the people with clipboards ask as they jotted down notes on the forms in front of them.

—"Do you have any open wounds?"

— "Let's take a look at that cut on your foot. Were you walking in water for a long period of time? It looks like it might be infected."

— "What medication do you take for that?"

— "When was the last time you were tested for tuberculosis?"

The new arrivals were grouped into smaller lines, depending on their answers to the questions.

"It's a little yellow pill," said a stooped older woman, "that one I take for my blood pressure. It comes in a brown bottle, but I can't exactly tell you the name of it."

"Don't worry. We'll figure it out," the Red Cross worker answered calmly. Courtney relaxed a little at the friendly tone of the volunteers and the obvious competence of the medical staff around him. His people would be in good hands here.

As he turned to walk back to the line, he caught movement out of the corner of his eye and looked up to see someone waving to him through the door of the Dome. The reflection on the glass made it difficult to identify the person until he came through the door. It was Troy Moody, a friend who stayed near him at Fischer, on the first floor by the breezeway in 1B. Courtney waved back and Troy came through the doors and down the steps.

"Man, I'm glad to see you," he said, punching Courtney lightly on the shoulder, "How'd you get here?"

"It's a long story," Courtney answered. "I'll tell you later."

"Streets, your Grandmama was asking me today if I saw you after the storm or knew where you went. I told her I didn't know where you—"

"My Grandmama!" Courtney interrupted him, grabbing his arm. "Where'd you see my Grandmama?"

"She's here, man. She's inside, right through them doors."

Courtney grabbed Troy's other arm and shook him—hard. "Is she okay? She ain't hurt or nothin'?"

"Naw, man, ease off, she's fine. I just talked to her a little bit ago."

"Are you sure it was my grandmamma?"

"Sure, man, I been knowing Miz Geraldine all my life."

Courtney leaned weakly against a lamppost. Was it possible he'd driven the bus to the exact place his grandmother had evacuated to? He turned and forced his rubbery legs to move. As he charged up the steps toward the front of the building, a large man in uniform stepped in front of the airport style metal detectors and blocked his way.

"I need to see your identification card," the security guard told him.

"I just got here. I don't have any kinda card yet."

"I'm sorry, son. You'll have to get back in line."

"But my Grandma's in there. I've got to see my Grandma."

"You can't enter the building until you've been processed. Your grandmother will be there when you get there."

Courtney looked back at the long line and groaned.

"It's okay, Streets," Troy caught up to him. "You wait here. I'll go get her for you. She can come out here."

Courtney sat on a nearby step and rubbed his throbbing temples. In the sudden release of tension, his head ached like a basketball was expanding inside his brain. He considered asking the Red Cross employee nearby if she had any pain reliever, but he didn't want to look like a junkie.

In spite of the pressure inside his head, he started smiling— smiling like he'd scored the game winning three-pointer. His grandmother was safe! She was safe and dry, well fed and cared for, clean and comfortable.

As much as he'd tried to think positive thoughts, he had personalized every story he'd heard on the bus. In the dark,

116

desperate reaches of his subconscious, he'd tried not to see the mental image of her body floating in the water or hear her screams for help as the water rose. When he heard the stories from the people behind him as he drove, it was her clothing he saw beneath the rubble and her hand reaching out to him. He shut the terrible pictures out of his head now, the ones he'd been determined to suppress. Troy's words erased them.

His Grandmama was safe! She was safe and dry and well fed. He'd found her unharmed and she was asking for him.

Thank you, God, thank you, thank you, he prayed while he waited, *I ain't asking for anything else for a long, long time. I don't know how to thank you for taking care of Grandma Streets. I just don't know what I'd do if something happened to her. You helped me find a place for my people, and now you're giving me back my Grandmama. I don't deserve all the things you do for me, but I'm gonna try real hard to be a good person.*

Finally, she was there—Grandma Streets, arms outstretched, smiling, and hugging him. He jumped to his feet, reached down and wrapped his arms around her, lifting her off the ground. He buried his face in her soft, white hair and fought to keep his emotions in check.

"What are you doing here?" she asked, looking up at him in genuine surprise after he set her down beside him. She didn't seem at all worried.

"What do you mean, what am I doing here?" he asked, miffed at her casual tone. "What are *you* doing here?"

"I thought you went with your dad." Damon Williams, Courtney's father, had dropped in and out of Courtney's life after he split up with Courtney's mom, sometimes spending a Saturday with his son, then disappearing for months at a time. Their relationship was rocky, but it was true Courtney had talked with him on the phone the day before Katrina hit. Miz Gerry must have heard him.

"No, I was staying over by Jamie's house. I came home after the storm to find you and you were gone. Ma, I was so worried about you. Why didn't you leave me a note?"

"Because I didn't know you were coming back. I thought I heard you tell Damon you were going with him."

"No. I didn't go anywhere with my dad. I called him the day before the storm, but he was already in the car leaving."

"How'd you get here?"

"With Gus and his family." She paused. "How did you get here?"

"Um, I got me a ride," he told her. Courtney looked down at his shoes, then out toward the street, careful not to look in the direction of the bus. "With, ah, some friends." She eyed him suspiciously.

"Have you done something you had no business doing, boy?" she asked him. "How come you're shaking?"

"I ain't shakin'."

"Yes, you are."

"It's just 'cause I was so scared something happened to you, and I'm so happy to find you."

doesn't tell her about the bus

"Look at me. Let me see your eyes. I can always tell when you're lying to me by how much you blink."

Courtney held his eyes comically wide, trying not to blink. "I'm straight, Grandma Streets. Don't worry 'bout me. I'm just glad you're okay."

She gave a dissatisfied grunt to let him know he hadn't fooled her; then she changed her approach. "What've you had to eat?" Her usual question. Feeding him was one of her favorite pastimes.

"Nothin'," he said, "but I'm ah'right."

"You get on in here and get you some pizza," she said, pulling him toward the door.

"They won't let me come in 'till I stand in this line," Courtney told her, "They said I gotta get some lil' piece of paper first."

118

"Then I'll bring some food out here to you," she said and hurried off.

Courtney sat down on the steps to wait for her. He was weak-kneed with relief that his grandmother was safe, but he had to admit that he was just a little hurt she hadn't found him before she left town. She could have called Jamie's cell phone to let him know she was leaving. And his Dad could have offered to pick him up. It seemed that everyone figured Courtney could take care of himself, now that he'd lived on his own for months. But there were times when he just wanted to be treated like a kid, to have someone look out for him, worry about him, and take care of him. Having everyone assume you could make it alone made him feel – well, alone. He wanted people to think of him as part of the constellation of their family, not as a satellite.

As he sat with his head in his hands, Troy Moody came toward him. He'd been talking with some of the people he knew from Fischer.

"Man, that was something—what you did with that bus," Troy said. The others had been filling him in on their adventure.

"Nothing you wouldn't have done too if you had you a bus," Courtney cut off his praise, glad to be interrupted by the reemergence of his grandmother with pizza. He saw her looking out over the crowd for him, and he waved at her.

"I could only get one piece for now, but I'll get you some more when you get inside. And I brought you some water too." Courtney felt guilty for feeling like she'd left him. The truth was, Grandma Streets had spent all of his life looking after him.

She sat with Courtney on the steps as he ate. He was surprised at his own lack of interest in food. In spite of his empty belly and the sounds it had made earlier, he was still too wired with nervous energy to think about eating.

"All right, come on out with it, Courtney Streets," Miz Geraldine told him. She used his nickname very rarely and only to lighten a tough situation. "I know something's going on."

"Don't get mad when I tell you this," Courtney said, leaning forward to see her eyes in the shadows cast by the bright lights above them. "You know I try not to do anything you'd be ashamed of."

"It's not me you've got to answer to. You just remember when God comes, you can't run," she said, gazing back. "Go on, I'm listening."

"Okay, you see that big bus parked by that curb over there?"

"I see it," she said.

"Well, I drove it here. That's how me and all these people got here from Fischer."

"You drove that bus?"

"Yes, ma'am."

"That bus right over there?"

"Yes, ma'am."

"With a bunch of people from the project?"

"Bout 200."

She sat back and cocked her head at him.

"Boy, you better get outta my ear telling tales like that."

"I'm fuh real, Grandmama. I'm telling you the truth."

"What're you talking about, Courtney? You don't know how to drive a bus."

"I do now," he said.

"Where'd you learn how to drive?" she asked, and he realized he hadn't exactly told her about the times his uncles and friends let him drive.

She waited for his answer.

"Video games," he looked at her without cracking a smile.

"You're playing with me now," she said, slapping his arm.

"No Ma, I'm serious."

"You brought 200 people here on a bus?"

"Yes, ma'am."

"Where are they now?"

"They're in line talking to the people from the Red Cross. Are you mad at me?"

"You're really telling the truth, aren't you?"

"Yes, ma'am, I am. Did I do the right thing?"

Then she sat completely still in that quiet way of hers, listening intently as he described the bus trip to Lafayette. He told the truth, but carefully edited out the part about the police roadblock. She didn't have to know everything.

She showed no surprise, nodding her head each time he told of picking up more passengers. Geraldine Miles was known for her calm personality and the same quiet, humble exterior that Courtney had inherited from her. Calm, cool, and collected; that's what people said about her. She was as cool as the other side of the pillow—smooth and unruffled. He finished and waited for her response as she turned his story over in her head.

"Well, it's a good thing you did, but a bad thing, too," she said finally. "There's always two sides to every story."

"Will the police arrest me?" He made himself voice his worst fear.

"I don't think so," she said gently. "But I can't say for sure." She never sugar coated anything. "You did what you had to do, Courtney. No sense looking back." She reached over and patted him, her hand like a child's on top of his large one. They sat in silence and watched the crowd around them.

"Mama, it's hot out here," Courtney said after a while. "Why don't you go on back in? I'll come and find you soon as I finish with this stuff they want me to do, but it might take a 'lil while." He reached in his pocket and felt the key to the bus.

She thought it was the right thing to do

He held out his hand to help her up from the curb. "You come find me when you get in. Even if I'm asleep, you wake me up. I wanna know when you're done here."

Courtney was far from done, but she had no idea what he was planning.

"Don't worry about me. I'm good. That pizza was just what I needed. Thank you."

She kissed him on the cheek and turned back toward the Cajundome; Courtney set out to look for Troy Moody again. He was still with Tom Wilson, about halfway down the line of people. He walked over to where they were standing.

"Troy, if my Grandma comes looking for me, just tell her I'm around here someplace, that you just saw me," he said. "I'll be back in a couple of hours."

"Streets, where you going?" Troy asked.

"I'ma go back to get them other people."

"What other people?"

"All them people on the Expressway I told I was coming back."

"Are you crazy?"

"I promised them."

"You serious?" Tom asked.

"Yeah, I had it in my heart from Jump Street I was going back, as soon as I saw them walking. I can't leave them there on the highway with nobody to help them."

"Why don't you just let it go, Streets?" Troy said. "You just saved over half of Fischer. You don't have to do this."

"I'm not a quitter, Troy. I'ma finish what I started."

His dad, in the limited time he spent with Courtney, drilled it into him—to finish what he started. Damon could be domineering, and Courtney was not accustomed to answering to this man who came around whenever he felt like it to order him around. On one particular weekend, his dad came and got him from his grandmother's apartment in the project. Courtney was hiding because he didn't want to play football.

Looking back, he may have been hiding because he was afraid. A few days before, he and his friends had gathered to play football in a vacant lot on Hendee and gunshots rang out. All of them scattered in terror, not knowing which direction the shooting was coming from. Later he heard that a man had been killed near where they'd been playing.

From the bedroom upstairs, he could hear the conversation between his grandmother and his father.

"Leave the boy alone," she said. "You can't make him like football."

"You can't protect him. Not this time, Miz Gerry. He's quit two times already, and I don't want my son to be a quitter."

Courtney heard him and moved toward the bedroom door to listen. He had, in fact, signed up for football and then quit—twice. Maybe his dad was right. Maybe he was a quitter. Was this how it started for those guys who hung out around the neighborhood with nothing to do because they couldn't hold onto a job? If he gave up football again, maybe he'd wind up like them, selling drugs on the street corner because they quit school and quit work and quit hope for a better life.

He opened the door the rest of the way and walked slowly out of the bedroom and down the stairs. His father smiled and patted him on the back as he got into the car, football gear in hand. He played that night, and scored both touchdowns in the championship game of North against McDonald Park.

"The cops ain't gonna let you back into Algiers." Troy told him now. "What you gonna tell them when they stop you?"

"Guess I'll figure that out if it happens."

Thomas Wilson spoke up, "I'm going with you."

Courtney looked at him in surprise. "You sure about that? You know you don't have to."

"I know. I want to go."

"If that's what you want, I have to admit I'd be glad for some comp'ny."

"Man, you're both crazy," Troy told them. "It's almost 11:00. It'll be way after midnight when you get back. You could at least wait until tomorrow."

"And then that whole group of people's got to spend the night on the side of the highway with them babies and children when they could be sleeping here where it's clean and comfortable. Naa, man, I'm going back now."

"How much gas we got left?" Tom asked.

"Plenty. That tank must hold a lot 'cause it was still on three quarters full when we pulled up."

"Then we're all set," Tom said.

"Let's do it." Courtney held up the key. And the two of them walked toward the bus.

"We got us a lil' more room now, Thomas," Courtney looked around as they boarded the empty bus. He stretched his tired limbs, sat down, and cranked the engine.

"Yeah," Tom grinned and took a seat in the first row. "It feels kinda good to sit down."

Chapter 12 – Miles to Go Before I Sleep

Courtney pulled away from the curb, looking back over his shoulder at the people he was leaving behind.

"You didn't tell your Grandma you were going back?" Tom asked.

"What do *you* think?"

"I think Miz Gerry would've had herself something to say about that."

"I think you're right. I'll find her when I get back to the dome."

They drove toward the entrance ramp for Highway 90, but this time it was 90 East. It seemed strange to Courtney to travel the same route they'd just taken, only backwards. Their destination was more certain this time, but the success of this rewind mission seemed more questionable.

"Hey, you did a pretty good job of driving this bus," Tom said, watching him turn the big steering wheel. "You don't have a license, do you?"

"No, man—never had a car, didn't need no license."

"How'd you learn how to drive?"

Courtney was becoming accustomed to this question. "My uncle's car...my friends...," he looked over slyly at Tom, "...and them cars we stole." There was complete silence for several seconds. Courtney held a perfect deadpan expression as Tom looked over at him, then he started laughing. The tension of the last few hours left his face and his eyes sparkled as he enjoyed the trick he'd played on his friend.

"I'm just messin' with you, Tom. I ain't never stole a car." He paused. "Well, not 'til today anyway."

"Man, I can't ever tell when you're jokin'," Tom complained, a little put out.

Courtney loved to kid people. At school he liked to reach down to swipe people's caps off their heads. None of them could catch him as he ran off with them, and he kept them for weeks at a time, amassing a collection of caps until he grew tired of the game and gave them back.

He also loved to walk up to a buddy who had a bottled drink, ask for a sip, then put his mouth all over it so they wouldn't want it back and would go buy another one. He walked down the halls at school once in big black clown shoes and had been talked into singing "Ford Truck Man" on stage at a Pep Rally to entertain his friends. The serious expression he wore most of the time hid his playful nature from people who didn't know him well. His smile was slow at first but spread across his entire face until his dark eyes danced wickedly at whatever prank he'd pulled off. His only rival for sly tricks among his friends was Reginald with his convincing storytelling and devious jokes. When the two of them got together, it was always a good time.

"That's 'cause I'm a Gemini," he told Tom now. "I got two sides to my personality."

His mother was a Gemini, too, but her two personalities split in a way that was something entirely different. It had taken him years to admit to anyone what life was like when her usually loving

126

personality turned unexpectedly into outbursts of rage. He thought back now to his conversation with Jamie on the day he told her what growing up with Gabriel had really been like.

She had asked him before about the scars she traced across his body with her fingers, but it was many months before he was ready to tell her the truth about his childhood. Finally he felt he could tell her—he wanted to tell her—something he'd never shared with anyone else.

She looked at him in shock when he said it for the first time.

"This is where your mother hit you?" she asked, stunned.

"Yeah, she beat me pretty good sometimes," he said, looking straight into her eyes.

"Oh, baby. I didn't know," she whispered. "Can you talk about it?"

"I can to you. I want you to know—everything."

"What kind of things did she beat you for?" Jamie asked quietly.

"In sixth grade she whipped me for the way I wrote my name on my papers at school." There was no self-pity in his voice. These were facts that had become a part of who he was. "She hit me over and over again because I made the loop at the bottom of the "C" instead of at the top."

"Oh, Courtney, I'm so sorry. I had no idea. She just seems so sweet whenever I'm around."

"You know, she can be. She's a good person. You saw how she takes people into our house who don't have anywhere to live – homeless people, sick people, people addicted to drugs that ain't got nowhere to stay. She treats them like family when their people give up on them. She takes care of them and cooks for them... "

He smiled at the memory of the way she'd fill the house with the smell of her favorite soul foods—bell peppers and cabbage, cornbread, and chicken, as she danced in the kitchen to her favorite rhythm and blues singers.

(margin note: told Jamie that his mom beat him)

bipolar

But then, he told Jamie, without warning, the rhythm of their lives would be interrupted by the blues that were always just under the surface. When her failures and frustrations pulled her into the dark place, Gabriel's "evil Gemini twin" was terrifying. Her rages, when they came, were wild and uncontrollable, and Courtney was usually the victim. All of her disappointment, guilt, fear, and sadness were directed at the easiest target—her son.

"There was no way to know when it was coming," he spoke in a soft, even voice. "Most days she was like the Angel Gabriel, and then some little thing would set her off and she'd lose control. She'd start hitting me and hitting me and hitting me."

Jamie stroked his face as tears filled her eyes. They'd been going out for over a year and he'd never said a word. "What did she hit you with?" Jamie asked carefully.

"Sometimes sticks and tree branches she brought in from the yard. Some of them were little and sometimes they were bigger ones that left cuts across my legs and drew blood."

"Did anyone else know?"

"Naa, I wore my school uniforms with the long sleeves and long pants even when it was hot so nobody could see the marks she left." He looked away from Jamie, focused on a spot on the wall, and steadied his voice.

"Nobody at school ever noticed?"

"After the worst times, I'd be walking with a limp for a day or two. One of my teachers asked me some questions one time when it hurt too bad to hold a pencil at school the next day, but I just told her I hurt my hand in basketball."

"Is that why you have trouble with your wrist sometimes?" Jamie had noticed that he rubbed his left wrist unconsciously when he was nervous or tired.

"Yeah, it mostly hurts if I have to do push-ups. That was the worst day, the day she hurt my wrist."

"Tell me about it, Courtney, I want to know what happened."

Jamie is the only person that knows

It was a day Courtney would never forget. He was 12 years old. She was standing at the stove cooking...

"Courtney, don't eat any more chips," his mom calls out to him. "Dinner's almost ready."

She walks into the living room where he's playing video games and stands behind him, watching.

"You hear me, Punkin?"

"Yes'm. What you cookin', Mama?" He asks without looking up.

"I made you a special meal for that good report card," she says, reaching down to hug him. "Fried chicken, black-eyed peas, yams, collard greens — all your favorites."

"Sounds great."

"That's the best you can do after all my hard work in the kitchen?" She reaches down and starts tickling him. "You better show me some love, boy!"

Courtney giggles and tries to squirm away from her. "I love you, Mama, I love you. Stop. I said I love you.

She holds him in a tight hug. "My little Honor Roll student," she says. "My little basketball star. I'm so proud of you."

Courtney grins, reveling in the attention. "What are you playing?" she asks.

"Zelda. You want to play?"

"I got a few minutes while things are cooking. Move over, big guy."

"Here, Mama, you take this one." He hands her the controller.

He tries to hold back, but after a few minutes of play, his score moves ahead of hers. Suddenly they hear the sound of a pot boiling over on the stove. Gabriel jumps up and runs to turn it down, then returns.

"What did you do?" she asks, looking at the screen.

"I didn't do nothin'," he answers, bewildered.

"You did. You cheated while I was gone."

"I didn't cheat," Courtney says, becoming wary. "I was already beating you. See? I won."

Gabriel moves closer to look at the screen.

"I didn't cheat, Mama. I had you by 50 points. See, 'Game Over.'"

"Game over?" She smacks him on the side of his head, playfully—but too hard.

"Oh, you think you're so smart? You think you're smarter than your mama?" She hits him again, harder.

"You think you know more than I do? You think I'm stupid, don't you?" She hits him again, hard enough to knock him to the floor.

"No, Mama. I don't think that."

"You cheated; that's how you beat me. You beat me because you cheated." The blow this time is violent enough to cause a bright flash in his head.

"I'm not going to have a son who cheats. I won't have another cheater in this house."

Courtney looks around the room wildly for an escape route but she is blocking him in. "No, Mama. I didn't cheat, I promise. I didn't cheat."

"Don't lie to me, boy. I can't stand a man who lies."

She reaches for the heavy two by four that slides into metal brackets to bolt the apartment door from the inside at night. It stays propped beside the door when not in use and is always within easy reach.

"Don't hit me, Mama! I'll be good. I promise." He is crying now. "Don't hit me." She swings and he throws his arms up to protect his head but he feels a searing pain shoot through his left wrist.

"Lying. Cheating. You're just like all the rest of them," she rages. "I didn't raise you to be a liar and a cheat. Do you hear me?"

Courtney cowers on the floor, trying to ward off the blows and crying out to her, but she always has trouble stopping once things have progressed this far.

Courtney broke off when he looked back at Jamie for the first time since he'd started telling her about that day. "Oh, baby, don't cry. I shouldn't have told you alla that."

"No," Jamie said. "I want to know all of it. I want you to tell me."

130

"It's okay. I'm fine now. It was a long time ago." He put his arms around her and pulled her to him. He held her for a few minutes, then pulled away to wipe his eye with his thumb.

"It just makes me so sad," she said. "Wasn't there anybody you could go to for help?"

"When it got really bad, I ran over to my grandmama's house, but I tried not to do that too much 'cause I didn't want her to worry about me."

"Did your mom leave you alone when you went to Miz Gerry's?"

"Mostly. She didn't usually follow me over there, but she did a couple of times, and then my grandma had to throw herself between us. She was begging her to stop. My mom, she was hard to control when she got like that but she most always listened to my grandma."

"I guess I've just never seen that side of her," Jamie said, still processing this new information.

"You know, that's why they call her 'Big Gabe', 'cause of her personality," Courtney said, "I've seen her throw herself at grown men, using her fists to settle her business. There ain't a lot of men, even, who can handle her. I guess that's one reason my dad left."

"You couldn't just stay over at your grandmama's?"

"I did spend the night there a lot. But I never knew when it was gonna happen. She could be in a good mood all day, joking and having fun, and then she would just change—just like that."

Courtney's eyes turned dark at the memory of evenings that began with laughter and ended with hot tears. On days when she seemed quiet, he moved silently through the house, keeping his distance and trying not to invite unwanted attention. Sometimes months would pass without incident, but then she would turn on him again, unloading her anger in a fit of violence. It seemed like a twisted catharsis; she transformed her emotional pain into a physical pain he was almost willing to carry if he thought it could

ran & stayed at his grandma's when it got bad

ease her. He tried so hard to please her, but there was no predicting what would set her off.

He looked away from Jamie's face, and his voice hardened. "She beat me for beating her at a video game."

Jamie listened quietly without comment.

"I tried to tell myself it was my fault when she punished me for something I'd done wrong. I wanted to believe it was her way of showing love, that she wanted me to grow up to be a good man, you know what I'm saying? But you tell me, how could I make excuses for her beating over losing a video game? What was the lesson I was supposed to learn from that?"

He bent his head and swiped his thumb and forefinger across his eyes, toward his nose.

Jamie took his other hand in both of hers. "You never went to a doctor when she hurt you?" she asked.

"No, there were a couple of times when I should have, but I didn't want to get her into trouble. I knew she didn't mean to do it."

"Did she ever apologize after? Did she say she was sorry?"

"No, she'd buy me stuff. I'd come home from school and there'd be a new shirt, a CD I'd been wanting. After the worst nights, she bought me new basketball shoes. I knew she was trying to make it up to me."

"Why didn't you tell me...before?"

"It's not something I like to talk about. I always kept thinking she'd change, that if I pulled my grades up and made something of myself, I could set an example for her and she'd try to get help. But it seemed like whatever I did was never enough. I told my Grandmama that no matter how hard I tired, my Mama was always mad at me."

"What did Miz Gerry say?"

"She said my Mama wasn't mad at me. She was mad at herself."

Jamie pulled his hand to her face and kissed it.

132

"I thought I could help her change, but I figured out all I could do was put her in God's hands. I pray for her every morning, and she's always the last thing I talk with God about before I go to bed every night."

He sighed and straightened his shoulders.

"I still love my mama. Lots of people had it worse than I did, growing up. When my mom was in a good mood, it was always Platinum Plus, but when it was bad, it was really bad."

Courtney had almost stopped hoping things would be different when she got out of jail next time. He kept thinking that—

"Look out, Streets!" Tom's cry interrupted his thoughts.

Courtney slammed on the brakes and the bus lurched. A National Guardsman had appeared out of nowhere and was stepping into the middle of the road. He was waving them over.

"I didn't know if you saw him," Tom said.

"I see him," Courtney said, keeping his voice calm. The soldier's Jeep was parked on the side of the road and he stepped in front of the bus. Courtney took a deep breath. He tried not to engage in the "help me" prayers many people used only in emergencies; instead he worked at maintaining a "connectedness" to God that enabled him to listen at all times. The Bible called it "praying without ceasing." His grandmother called it being "prayed up."

"What're you gonna tell him?" Tom asked as the soldier walked toward them.

"I'm gonna tell him the truth."

"Man, that's a big 'ole gun he's carrying." Tom's voice was shaky.

Courtney rolled to a stop and opened the bus door. The uniformed Guardsman stepped to the doorway and looked at the two boys inside. He was a beefy young guy with a shaved head and a serious expression. Courtney realized he wasn't much older than they were.

"Where do you think you're going?" he asked gruffly. "This road is closed. You're not supposed to be driving on it."

"My lil pahdner here and me, we're going back to pick up some people we left on the side of the road, sir." Courtney spoke courteously and looked the man straight in the eye.

"What people?" the soldier asked.

"Some people we passed when I was taking another group up to Lafayette. I promised them I'd come back for them—after I dropped off the rest of the folks I had on my bus. We were too full to pick them up."

The soldier studied the two boys and said nothing.

"I'm just gonna pick them up right down this road a ways," Courtney continued, his soft tone confident, as if permission had already been granted, "and then turn around and bring them back to the Cajundome where I left the other people."

The soldier's eyes narrowed and his jaw clenched. Courtney watched him, trying to read his face. He could feel Tom tensed up behind him but he kept his eyes on the man who had the power to shut down his plan. The seconds ticked away as they waited.

Finally the soldier sighed and said, "I don't know why I'm doing this. It's not a good idea...but just make it quick. You're going straight there and straight back?"

"Yes, sir," Courtney said.

"All right then, move it."

"Thank you, sir." Courtney smiled.

"Thank you," echoed Tom.

The man waved them on as he stepped back and Courtney rolled forward slowly.

"I can't believe he didn't stop us," Tom said. "He didn't even ask you for your license. We got lucky."

"That was *nothin'* but God right there. Truth is, I knew he was gonna let me roll with it," Courtney answered. "And if he didn't, we'd be looking for another way. I wasn't going to give up, not for nobody."

After they pulled back onto Highway 90, the empty road stretched ahead of them. There were a few cars here and there on their return journey, but the two boys were mostly alone on the expressway. There wasn't much to see now that it was dark, so Courtney felt more focused on the road. He knew he should have been tired, but he felt keyed up, and staying awake took no effort. They rode in silence for a while, each lost in his own thoughts about the events of the day.

"You ever play basketball there?" Courtney asked Tom as they drove past the Alario Center heading back into the city.

"Oh, yeah," Tom said, "but not as much as you, probably."

"AAU basketball kept me out of trouble. I think I woulda had a lot more time to get into stuff I wasn't s'posed to if I hadn't been playing ball. I was so blessed with coaches who took an interest in me. AAU ball gave me a focus, you know what I mean?"

Tom nodded.

"Only vacations I ever had. They took us in vans to the games—beaucoup games. They even flew us to Las Vegas and Orlando—for tournaments. I never woulda thought I'd get to go to Disneyworld, but basketball took me places I never woulda seen."

"How many years did you play?"

"Um, from about age eleven to about thirteen."

"Hey, did you ever see the Hornets practice there?"

"Naa, but they came to my school once—talked to us about setting goals and working to achieve your dreams. That's when I decided I want to play in the NBA one day. It's all I ever wanted to do."

"I hear you, man. You gonna invite me to some of your games?"

"Sure, Tom. We'll be chilling with Kobe and driving around Miami in my new Ferrari with Beyonce," Courtney smiled broadly at the thought. "Or maybe Paris Hilton. Or maybe Britney Spears. I haven't given up on Britney. I believe in giving people another chance."

His smile faded as he thought about what the hurricane meant to his career goals. "If schools don't reopen after this storm, there ain't gonna be any NBA."

"Why d'you say that?"

"If I lose my senior year of basketball, it ain't gonna matter how well I played in my first three years of high school. Man, you know recruiting decisions are based on that last year. It's what you do senior year that makes the difference. They want to see how you matured and what you can bring to the college program."

"But you were playin' great junior year."

"'Bout 17 points a game, but it don't matter. All of those players at other schools are gonna be pouring it on for college coaches, and nobody's gonna see me play. My name'll be lost in the system. There's was no way anybody's gonna offer me a scholarship based on just my junior year alone. And if I don't have a strong college program to show what I can do, there's no way I can make it to the NBA." Courtney tried to keep the bitterness from his voice.

"But they know who you are already. Did you go to any of them summer camps at colleges?"

"Naa, I know Coach Moore got some letters inviting me to go to some. But he didn't ever tell me about them."

"How come?"

"I don't know. I just figure if he kept 'em from me, he had a good reason."

"How do you know you got invited?"

"One of my friends saw letters on his desk and read 'em when he was out of his office. All I know is I trust the man. He wouldn't never do me wrong."

Courtney grew quiet, then nodded toward the state park they were passing, "Bayou Segnette—lotta good times there—alla them school field trips when we were little. Man, I loved that wave pool."

"Me, too," Tom said.

"We used to have picnics there—with the whole class. Saw some armadillos, and a hawk one time. Heard there was an alligator, but we never saw him."

"Yeah, it's kinda messed up that you can fish for fresh water and salt water fish in the same place," Tom said. "Means something's wrong if the ocean can get all the way up here, you know what I'm sayin?"

"I don't know, man." Courtney shook his head.

"Hey, Streets, you okay? You're not sleepy?"

"I'm good," Courtney answered. "I can't really say why, but I'm not even a 'lil bit tired."

As they drew closer to Algiers, there was more activity than when they'd passed this way on the first trip—people running across a parking lot down to the right, below the expressway.

"Look at that—people stealing cars!" Courtney nodded toward the Dodge dealership. A police car was swinging into the car lot as they passed, lights flashing and siren blaring.

"Over there, too. They're taking stuff from Burlington," Tom added, pointing to two men carrying loads of clothing from the front of the store. Another police car was following a third man who was running through the street on foot.

"People are going *crazy* around here," Tom said.

Courtney sighed. "This storm's turned people into something else."

"They're just grabbing stuff up," Tom said.

"We got trouble up ahead too." Courtney nodded toward another National Guard truck blocking their way.

"This ain't good," Tom said. "They're gonna think we been stealing stuff too. Man, they're 'bout to take us to *jail*."

"They're not gonna take us to jail," Courtney said, praying silently, *Please, God, don't let them take us to jail.*

Courtney hoped for a replay of his last National Guard encounter as the soldier approached his bus, but this man was older and looked stern and serious. "This road is closed," he said as he walked up to the door of the bus Courtney opened. His tone and posture were intimidating. "No one's supposed to be driving on it."

"We just need to pick up some people and then we'll be outta here. We're trying to help some people who don't have any way outta the city."

"Sorry, but you're going to have to turn this thing around. I have my orders."

"Please, sir. I promised those people I'd come back for them. They're walking down the highway with little babies and children, and if I don't go back for them, they're gonna have to sleep on the side of the road. They got nothing to eat and no place to stay and I'ma take them to the Cajundome where I left the other people from the project. I give you my word I'll get outta here soon as I pick them up."

It was a long speech for Courtney. He knew he would lose time if he had to turn around and find another way in. And every minute he lost left people stranded on the side of the road. The guardsman pushed his cap back a little on his head and wiped sweat from his forehead. He looked from Courtney to Tom and back again.

"They're just right down this road, about a mile from here," Courtney added. He felt the steel blue eyes boring a hole through him, but he refused to look away. His heart sank at the stern expression he faced and the grim mouth set in a hard line. A nagging voice in his head told him this might be the end of the line—the point where his mission ended in a jail cell.

Suddenly, the man replaced his cap, relaxed his rigid stance just a little and shook his head, "Man, you guys are crazy. If the wrong National Guard guys stop you, they're gonna handcuff you and put you in jail. Do you know where that is right now? It's the Greyhound bus station, and you do *not* want to be there."

"No sir, we do not," Courtney said while Tom shook his head in agreement.

"Alright then, do what you've gotta do, and then get on out of here."

"Yes, sir. Thank you, sir." Courtney was already closing the bus door before the soldier changed his mind. He smiled as the bus rolled forward.

"Man, I thought that was it." Tom let out his breath. "I thought that dude was gonna take us in."

"Nothing's gonna stop me now," Courtney said. "Help me keep an eye out, Tom. I think we're getting close to where we saw them. Wasn't it around S.Jamie by that light?"

A few minutes later, Tom spotted them—the small crowd they'd seen earlier. Most of them were sitting on the ground, leaning against each other. A couple of men seemed to be standing guard.

"There they are—over across from that Shell station. They're right where we left 'em!"

"They must have decided not to walk on the highway at night," Courtney said. "That was a good move."

One of the men saw the yellow bus and started waving for them to stop. His shouting attracted the attention of the others in the group and within seconds, they were all on their feet, yelling and waving. One woman began to run across the highway toward them.

"Don't do that," Courtney said under his breath. He yelled out the window, "I'm coming. I just gotta turn around." He wasn't sure they could hear him, but he pointed to the exit sign ahead and called out, "Y'all wait 'till I get over there."

He pulled off at the next exit and circled back under the expressway to change directions. He drove up the ramp so he was headed west once again. When he pulled up next to them, the people started running toward him.

75 people loaded on

"You came back," a woman said in surprise.

"Yes, ma'am. I told you I wouldn't forget you," Courtney said as he helped her on board.

"Thanks, man." "God bless you." People greeted him as they climbed on board. "My baby's so tired."

They filed down the aisle and collapsed into the seats, moving toward the windows to make more room. Courtney estimated about 75 of them, so they fit pretty well on the bus.

"How come you're not tired?" Tom asked him, yawning, as they pulled away with the grateful passengers.

"I don't know, but I'm good. We'll be there in no time."

Five minutes after they'd picked up their group, Tom pointed ahead in the darkness. "I think that's some more people waving at us."

Courtney pulled the bus over as about forty people converged on them. "I didn't even see this 'lil group on the way in. Did you?"

"No, I guess we were so busy watching those people stealing cars, we didn't even see 'em. They mighta been sittin' down so it was hard to see them in the dark."

2nd group (40 people)

After the second group loaded on, there were a little over one hundred riders, a full house by every-day standards but a light load after the 200+ crowd earlier in the evening.

The second trip to the Cajundome seemed much shorter now that he knew where he was going. The gas gauge still showed one quarter full when Courtney pulled into the parking lot. He guided it

140

made it to the dome

to the same spot on the curb, turned off the engine, and helped the tired travelers down the steps. Tom, waiting at the bottom of the steps, watched Courtney turn back, take a last look down the aisle, pat the steering wheel affectionately, and replace the keys in the ignition.

"You don't think you ought to keep the key?" he asked as Courtney stepped down beside him.

"What key?" Courtney looked straight ahead.

"The key to the bus."

"What bus?" Now Courtney looked at him as if genuinely puzzled.

"Oh... I get it." Tom smiled.

got inside the cajundome

Chapter 13 – The Cajundome

Even though it was 2:00 a.m., Courtney and Tom waited in line outside the dome for nearly two hours. When they finished with their physical screening and stepped inside, the security guard who stopped Courtney earlier eyed the badge Courtney now wore, made eye contact and smiled. They walked through the concrete hallways and saw that every side room and office was filled with people and their belongings. Most were asleep, but a few looked up at them as they passed. They stopped at a table where a young woman with a Red Cross handed out blankets and pillows.

"Courtney, come look at this," Tom called as he stepped over to the large open doorways to get a better view of the dimmed interior of the dome. On the floor below, hundreds of people were fanned out in a complicated quilt design of cots, mattresses, and blankets. Around them were tables of supplies and workers moving quietly about.

"It looks like a big old beehive," said Tom.

"'Cept all the bees are asleep."

"Not everybody's asleep," Tom said. They watched as Red Cross volunteers passed by them talking into walkie-talkies and carrying boxes, nurses with clipboards consulted doctors in lab coats, and police officers and National Guardsmen paced the hallways. The rhythms of the colony did not stop during the wee hours of the morning.

"It's like a little city," Courtney turned back to a dark haired Red Cross guy waiting to hand them individual packages of toiletries.

"Yeah, we've got a pharmacy, a barber shop, a bulletin board for job postings, church services—you name it."

"How many people you got in here?" Tom asked.

"A little over 9,000 right now. We're expecting double that many, the way they're coming in."

"Wish you had a basketball court," Courtney said.

"There's a goal outside. I think you could find a pick-up game most days," the guy answered.

Courtney remembered his promise to wake his grandmother when he made it inside the dome, but he decided to let her sleep. He was hoping she hadn't found out he went back into the city.

"Tom, look at that." Courtney nodded toward the huge monitor at the top of the Cajundome. CNN was replaying scenes from Hurricane Katrina.

Without electricity for television, it was their first look at pictures of the flooding taking place just across the river, and it was the first they knew of what had happened on the Gulf Coast. They stood mesmerized at the video footage of the devastation. They stared, trying to comprehend the videos of neighborhoods turned into lakes with rooflines barely visible.

There were blank slabs where houses once stood. There were sidewalks ending to nothing and steps that led nowhere.

They gazed in disbelief at steel girders twisted like pretzels and bridges buckled like Lego's.

There were steeples without churches, and everywhere – huge mounds of rubble. They saw bloated bodies floating in the flood waters, makeshift crosses made by grieving relatives, and families sobbing over missing children.

An occasional American flag draped over the debris reminded them they were watching the plight of their own countrymen, not some destitute population in a faraway land.

"Man, I knew it was bad," Courtney breathed, "but I didn't know it was *that* bad!"

"I ain't never seen nothing like that," Tom whispered.

The stood rooted to the spot, incredulous at the shocking scenes before them.

"Here you go." They had completely forgotten the Red Cross volunteer waiting to hand them each a small kit. "There's some toothpaste and deodorant and stuff you might need in there."

"Thanks," Courtney tore his eyes away from the television screen long enough to acknowledge him.

"They leave that thing on all night?" he asked gesturing toward the JumboTron TV.

"Yeah, a lot of people here have trouble sleeping, so it gives them something to do. Don't worry, they keep the volume low. You can pick up a cot from that stack over there. Just set it up anywhere you like. We just ask that you move quietly so you don't wake up people who are sleeping, since it is, um, you know, really late." He looked at his watch. "Or early."

Suddenly the screen was filled with a smiling face, a face Courtney knew well. He grabbed Tom's arm and pointed.

"Tom, look at that! It's Jabbar!"

"Shhh!" The Red Cross held up a hand in warning.

Courtney and Tom stared in amazement at the scene on the screen – Jabbar, being interviewed by a national news reporter! The text headline below him said Houston Astrodome.

"He made it, Courtney!" Tom said in a shout-whisper. "Jabbar went to Houston! He made it!"

Jabbar (2nd bus) made it to Houston + was interviewed by national news reporters

144

Courtney strained to listen, but the screen switched abruptly to other scenes outside the Astrodome.

"It's so low I couldn't hear it. Jabbar made it! Thank you, God! We did it. We got all of those people out."

"Nobody else was doing anything and you and Jabbar – you did it."

"And Nas, too. We had to try, you know. My coaches always told me you miss 100% of the shots you don't take." He turned to Red Cross guy. "How far is Houston from here?"

"Probably about five hours by car."

"They musta just got there."

"Wonder why he went to Houston," Tom said.

"I don't know. Maybe he knows somebody there."

"Jabbar on CNN! Jabbar—big timin' on national television," Tom laughed.

"Yeah, he did his thing. You know Jabbar wheeled that bus in there," Courtney said. "I bet he spunt it!"

They both knew how much Jabbar liked attention. Unlike Courtney, he was obviously enjoying the camera's focus on his adventure.

"I just hope he doesn't get us in trouble," Tom said. The two boys finally found a spot on the arena floor near and door and settled in for the night.

"I don't think I'm gonna be able to sleep," Courtney whispered as they stretched out on the cots. "I'm still too jacked up."

"It's gonna take some gettin' used to—sleeping in the middle of all these people. How long you think we're gonna be here?"

There was no answer.

"Courtney," Tom whispered. He looked over and saw that the exhausted bus driver was sound asleep.

fell straight asleep

The next morning, Courtney woke to find Nas standing over him.

"Hey, Courtney, there's a National Guard man asking questions about the bus out there," Nas told him.

"What'd you tell him?"

"Nothin'. He didn't ask me. He was just talkin' to other people."

"Anybody give him my name?" Courtney asked.

"I don't think so."

"You think we're gonna get arrested?" Tom asked, fully awake now and scrambling to his feet.

Suddenly someone turned up the volume on the Jumbotron and the voice of President Bush filled the room. "I think there ought to be zero tolerance of people breaking the law during an emergency such as this, whether it be looting, or price gouging at the gasoline pump, or taking advantage of charitable giving, or insurance fraud."

"I don't feel so good," said Tom, sitting back down on his cot.

"Don't worry, Thomas," Courtney said, "You're not in trouble. It's all on me. I'll take the blame for any kinda charges they want to put on me.

He waited all that day, pacing and watching the door, waiting for someone to come to take him away. In his head an imaginary tape played on a loop, a tape of the police escorting him in handcuffs to the squad car—just like he'd seen them escort his mother. He spoke to very few people and ducked his head every time someone in uniform passed him.

For the next three days in the Cajundome, he felt his heart race each time he looked up and saw a National Guardsmen or police officer enter the big arena. There was a strong police presence there; he was constantly on edge. He tried not to call attention to himself, tried to blend into the crowd. He hoped that

President Bush's "zero tolerance" policy didn't include his bus-borrowing caper.

"It's gone," he told Jamie when he was finally able to reach her on a borrowed cell phone. "The bus is gone. Somebody moved it."

"You think the police took it off?"

"I don't know, but I'm sure not gonna ask any questions."

"I miss you, baby," Jamie told him.

"I miss you, too. Where is Orange, Texas anyway?"

"Not too far from Houston."

"How long you gonna be there?"

"I don't know, Courtney. My mom really likes it here. A lot of people are looking for jobs in Texas because they don't have anything to go back to."

"I hate it—not knowing when I'll see you again."

"I know. Me, too."

"Is Rob still there?" she asked.

"No, he left with his mom to stay with his uncle in Baton Rouge. Nas is gone now too. It's just me and Thomas and Troy Moody."

"You doin' okay?" she asked.

"Yeah— a little restless, I guess."

"What do you do all day?" she asked.

"They got a basketball court outside; if the weather's okay, I'm always there. Some days I play video games with some of the little kids…and I look out for my Grandma. We been talking a lot about all the things that happened and what we're gonna do now."

"What *are* you gonna do?"

"Grandma Streets, she's wantin' one of them trailers they're giving out. She wants me to go to school over here when we get settled in a trailer."

"You could play ball there."

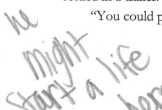

doesn't wanna live here

"I don't know. I don't even want to think about starting over someplace else with a new coach and guys I don't know."

"But some of the guys from Landry might be there."

"Yeah, maybe. We'll see." Courtney changed the subject. "The hardest part about being here is night time. It's pretty hard to sleep with about a thousand strange people all around you."

Most nights he was awake for hours, listening to the unfamiliar sounds that surrounded him—people snoring, coughing, whispering to crying babies, wheezing, or crying out in their sleep.

The place seemed pretty safe, in spite of rumors of a "raper-man" that brought extra National Guard soldiers in to beef up security. Still, children tossed in nightmares and adults moved quietly around the dome in congruent circles of insomnia.

The children's fear touched something deep inside Courtney. He watched them cling to their parents, unwilling to allow them out of their sight even for a minute to go to the bathroom.

They became nervous and afraid if the weather turned dark, and a thunderstorm could spark a terror that spread like a childhood rash through the building.

During the day he listened to people talking in small groups about their search for missing relatives and friends. Much of the day was taken up with frantic cell phone calls, addresses posted on bulletin boards and websites, and emails to anyone who might have information about the loved ones of the people at the Cajundome.

They also relived the events that led them to this point—to the loss of everything they owned. How had this happened to the city they loved? Some of them understood that politicians had, for years, allowed coastlands to be gouged by navigation channels and oil exploration. Salt from the encroaching ocean water had killed off everything, including the cypress trees in the swamps, making a bad situation worse.

They had seen federal plans to repair levees, build new floodwalls, and improve pumping stations scrapped by budget cuts

rumor of a raper

as costs for the war in Iraq mounted. Courtney's neighbors were left to wonder how much of a difference those projects might have made in the damage inflicted by the hurricane.

The balance of nature had been ignored by those who destroyed the wetlands to build commercial structures, and Katrina exacted a heavy penance. She lashed out like a spoiled child who finds her sand castle disrupted and then wrecks the entire structure in a fit of anger.

In an unholy tantrum of astonishing power, she smashed coastal homes into piles of rubble and kicked huge walls of water across cities and towns. Courtney was surrounded, day and night, by the people who had been punished for the greed of oil companies, developers and government officials.

He heard the personal stories of the people around him, too. There was no privacy in the Cajundome. With cots lined together like a bizarre multi-age summer camp, the intimate lives of strangers became public.

There was no need to eavesdrop; their voices filled his waking hours and echoed through his sleep. Not only was he aware of their losses from the storm, he knew how they looked and sounded as they slept, who they fought with on their cell phones, and what their health problems were.

Thousands of families had been separated by the storm. Some couples were split up when one spouse was needed to accompany an elderly or special-needs relative to medical centers, leaving another to care for the children alone. There were good days when he watched people being reunited with missing relatives—and bad days when someone found out a loved one didn't make it out of the flood.

They grieved together, not only for people, but also for family pets that weren't allowed in rescue boats. Because there was no plan for animal evacuation, many survivors were forced to leave them behind or worse, to watch them swim behind the boat until they couldn't keep up any more.

The animals that managed to stay alive were picked up weeks later, many of them starving and terrified, and taken to animal shelters.

But hundreds were never found by their owners.

The people in the Cajundome also grieved for sentimental [*been in here for a week*] possessions they left behind that represented family members long gone. They had lost important mementoes of a way of life that could never be restored. Courtney listened to their stories as he and his friends waited for news of school reopening.

"You heard anything about Landry?" Tom asked him after a week passed.

"No, I don't think they're gonna open back up," Courtney [*doesn't think the schools opening*] told him.

"But the school—we passed it. It didn't look like it had a lot of damage."

"I know, but there ain't gonna be anybody living there for a while. Too many people's houses got all torn up and the streets have got to be cleaned up, and there's probably not enough teachers left in town to run the school." L.B. Landry, they found out later, had become a base of operations for the National Guard and FEMA officials. Hundreds of emergency management officials set up camp there and at the U.S. naval base in Algiers because of its stone's-throw proximity to New Orleans. The old building, which needed three million dollars in repairs even before Katrina, would never be used again to house classrooms.

"So what're we gonna do about graduating?" Tom asked.

"I don't know, man. They've got to let us make it up. They know it's not our fault we're not in school."

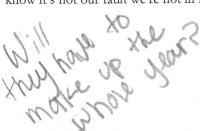

Will they have to make up the whole year?

"I think I might go down to Northside and check it out. There's a bus that picks people up here and I heard it's a good school."

"Yeah, my Grandmama wants me to see 'bout starting back to school here."

"How is Miz Geraldine?" Tom asked. "I ain't seen her in the past few days."

"She's good. She's keeping busy reading all the time."

"What's she reading?"

"Oh, you know, all them big old books she likes – the ones with no pictures."

"You talked to Jamie?"

"Yeah," Courtney sighed heavily, "she's been telling me I need to go to school too." He talked to Jamie several times each week. When it all came crashing down on him—the pain of losing his home, his friends, and maybe his chance to play college ball— she was the only one who could cheer him up. The sound of her voice made everything better.

He tried not to think about the fact that they no longer lived in the same town. He refused to focus on the uncertainties that faced them. Losing his senior year was heartbreaking, but losing Jamie too would be more than he could take right now.

Chapter 14 – FEMA Trailer

"They got us a trailer," his grandmother woke him one morning with the news. "We can finally move out of here tomorrow." He was irritated at being wakened early—until he saw how excited she was. They had waited patiently as family after family left the Cajundome for more permanent housing. They were some of the last people left. Every day Miz Geraldine asked when they would get their FEMA trailer, and every day they were told it would be soon.

"You know I'm grateful for everything they been doing for us at the Cajundome," he told Jamie on the phone, "but sleeping in a giant room with alla those other people is 'bout to drive me crazy."

"Are you still sleeping on that tiny little cot?" she asked, laughing at the thought of Courtney's long limbs hanging off the small frame he had described to her.

"No, Troy Moody's mom left me a mattress they had when she moved out. That's a whole lot better. It's just—you know—noisy. And I'm used to being by myself."

"Didn't you promise your grandmother you'd go back to school as soon as y'all had a place to live?" Jamie reminded him.

"I'm just worried you're going to get further behind if you don't go back." He didn't answer her, but he knew she was right.

The day they moved into the trailer, Miz Geraldine was practically dancing with excitement. They called a cab to deliver them and their few belongings to the trailer park.

"It's Number 27," his grandmother told the driver.

"The Red Cross man said the trailers are furnished," she said to Courtney as they drove away, "with beds and sofas—and they put in some sheets and towels to get you started. We've got that money from FEMA for food and cleaning supplies." Miz Gerry was already organizing their new home in her head. Months of living without any control of their schedule or surroundings had been hard on her.

Courtney smiled as he watched the Cajundome grow smaller in the taxi's rear view mirror. He had seen people who seemed almost afraid to leave the dome when other accommodations became available. They were so traumatized by the hurricane, they viewed the first safe haven they found as home. Anxious to avoid any more change in their lives, they held onto their small living space in the Cajundome as long as they were allowed to stay. Courtney, on the other hand, couldn't wait to get away.

He had received only $250 from the Red Cross for food and personal needs because he lived with his grandmother and she'd been given an allocation from FEMA. In the storm's aftermath people learned that—after the math—you got almost nothing. Courtney and Tom joked that not one penny of their FEMA money would go toward pizza. They had eaten it for lunch and dinner for weeks in the Cajundome. It would be a long time before they'd want anything with cheese or pepperoni on it.

"There it is," Miz Geraldine pointed to a trailer that looked exactly like the other fifty surrounding it. She was out of the cab almost before the driver stopped good.

Courtney helped the man unload the blankets and pillows and the few bags of clothing they had acquired at the Cajundome.

"You first, Grandma Streets," Courtney told her as he unlocked the door.

"Oh, my," she said as she stepped inside, "It's bigger than I thought it would be." Courtney followed close behind her. After the confines of a tiny corner of the Cajundome for weeks, the small trailer seemed unbelievably spacious. The living area had a kitchen that was outfitted with a basic table and two chairs. Through an open door toward the front, he saw a double bed and a small dresser.

"It's nice, "Miz Gerry said, "It's got a sofa and a big chair, and a kitchen table."

"Hey, I got my own bedroom," Courtney announced as he opened the second door into another bedroom. For the first time in weeks, he'd be able to just be by himself. He'd almost forgotten what that was like.

"We were lucky. I heard a lot of families got a one-bedroom," his grandmother said.

"Look at this—a shower we don't have to share with all those other people," Courtney said, reaching in and turning the faucet. He smiled at the things that now seemed like luxuries to him.

"Hot water heater's right here," Miz Geraldine was opening all the closets.

"It's got a microwave," Courtney called.

"And a pretty nice sized refrigerator," she said, joining him in the tiny kitchen.

Courtney watched her checking out the cabinets.

"Not too much storage space," she said.

"We ain't got much to store."

"I'll take care of that, just as soon as I can get to the grocery store. I brought us some stuff for sandwiches from that little store near the dome, but I'll get set up for cooking tomorrow." He knew she was anxious to reclaim the routines of their lives that centered around Creole food traditions—the little things like crusty French bread, Zatarain's mustard, and Community coffee with chicory— the ground root used since Civil War days when it was added to extend the brew during shortages. His people drank their coffee rich and dark, cut in half with scalded Pet milk and loaded with sugar. "Regulah" coffee meant cream and sugar added; only Yankees drank it black.

"Mmm-mm, I been missing your cooking."

"Well, I'll make up for lost time; Thanksgiving'll be here before you know it."

"Are we gonna have turkey *here*?"

"Why, sure. I've already talked to your uncles about coming. We don't have a lot of room, but we'll make do."

It was the first time he felt a glimmer of hope that one day they might return to some semblance of normalcy. If holiday traditions could be reclaimed, maybe their former lives hadn't been completely lost. That night they both slept well for the first time in weeks, in spite of their unfamiliar surroundings.

"The trailer sounds great," Jamie said on the phone the next day. "I'm so glad you were able to get out of the Cajundome."

"Me, too. If my Grandmama's happy, I'm happy," he told his girlfriend.

The day after they moved in, as promised, Courtney got up early, showered, and dressed for school. His grandmother was thrilled, but she was smart enough not to make a big deal of it. He watched nervously for the bus as he waited on the corner with other kids from the trailer park. There were a few he knew from the dome, but most were people he didn't recognize.

Northside High School was a plain brick building. Courtney got off the bus and walked up the sidewalk to the front door.

He fought back thoughts of his old school; walking into the door of another school building made it all real. He would never

misses his old life

wear the Landry blue and gold at graduation. He'd never own a tassel with LHS like the seniors who graduated before him. And he'd never see most of his friends again. One day they were sitting in class making plans for ball games and dances, and the next day they were scattered all across the country. He never even had a chance to say goodbye.

He walked slowly into the front office. The place was a flurry of activity and he waited, shifting his weight from one foot to the other, for someone to notice him. Finally a small older woman in glasses came over and peered up at him from behind the counter. "Can I help you?" she asked.

"I'm here to register for school," he said.

The woman eyed him suspiciously—or maybe she just had vision problems.

"We'll need a certified copy of your birth certificate, immunization forms, and proof of residency. Do you have a driver's license?"

"No, but I get asked that a lot." He smiled.

"If you don't have a driver's license, you can use a utility bill that verifies the parent or guardian's physical address." The woman seemed immune to his charm.

"Uh, I don't have a birth certificate," Courtney was about to explain but she cut him off.

"What school did you previously attend?" she asked. "We're going to need your records."

"L.B .Landry High School. That's in Algiers. My school, um, it ain't open for me to get my records."

"I see," she said. "So you have no documentation."

"I don't have any papers," Courtney raised his voice, exasperated. "See, there was this hurricane."

"Don't get smart with me young man; I'm just doing my job."

"I don't have anything," he reined in his anger. "I just got out with my clothes."

doesn't have anything she is asking for for school

156

"Okay. And your parents are now living where?"

"Well, my mama, she's in jail, and my dad, he moved to Denver, but I don't stay with him. I stay with my Grandmama." The woman frowned. Courtney was used to people stereotyping him – "from the projects," "mom in jail," "Dad moved away." He was always being graded on other people's performance. It didn't seem fair.

"And your grandmother—is she your legal guardian?"

"I don't know about legal, but she's my guardian." Courtney spoke with an elaborate patience he didn't really feel.

"If you're living with someone who is not your biological or adopted parent, that person must have full legal guardianship, through a certified court order by a state court or a state or federal agency, in order for them to register you for school."

"My Grandmama raised me while my mama's been in jail."

"And your current residence?"

"We're staying in one of those trailers they brought in. Number 27. Right offa Brothers Road."

"I'm sorry, but your grandmother will need proof of guardianship to register you for school here." The woman looked at him without blinking until he finally turned and walked out the door.

Courtney left the building, shoulders slumped, feeling as if he had somehow failed a test. He'd been sized up and found lacking. He wondered what he looked like to this woman. Was there something about him that made her feel he was a troublemaker? He knew other Landry kids who'd enrolled at Northside; they didn't have paperwork from the school. Her biggest problem seemed to be with proving his grandmother was his guardian. Maybe they didn't want him to register because he came in alone. He knew most of the other kids all had at least one parent with them.

Only got in trouble 1 time

He had never been in trouble at school, well—except for one
time. There was no way she could know about his expulsion in
seventh grade....was there?

He still couldn't think about that day—the one black mark on
his disciplinary record—without getting angry. He prided himself
on walking away from things he couldn't change, but this one was
hard to let go.

Courtney had walked into his first period class five minutes
after the morning tardy bell. Students were working at their seats
on an assignment on the board. Mrs. Addison, his seventh grade
science teacher, gave him a look as he slid into his desk.

He unzipped his backpack as quietly as he could and reached
inside it for his book. As he flipped to the page number written on
the board, the boy in front of him turned around and looked at
him. Several students near him sniffed the air. A couple of them
made faces.

"Man, you stink," a girl next to him muttered.

"You better get outta here," his cousin Rob hissed at him
from across the aisle.

Courtney froze. Rising above the chalky smell of the
classroom and the herbal odor of the kitty-litter disinfectant the
janitors spread on the floors at night was an unmistakable sweetish
tang. He leaned his face down to his sleeve and smelled his shirt.
He reeked of marijuana! He had walked into the school building
and taken a seat in the middle of science class smelling like a pot
party on Saturday night.

It wasn't his. He hadn't even touched it. He'd been walking to
school, running late as usual, when a car pulled up to the curb.
Three of the street guys he knew had offered him a ride to school.
Two of them were passing a joint and the pungent smoke filled the
car. It never occurred to him that the smell would linger on his
clothing this long. The smell of weed seemed to be wafting through

Smelled like weed

158

the classroom as another student turned to look at him, sniffing—
then another.

Trying not to be too obvious, Courtney desperately rubbed at
the sleeve of his uniform. The school's administration, in an effort
to minimize gang attire, required everyone to wear white polo shirts
and navy pants, which now seemed out of synch with the cannabis
cologne he was now sporting.

He had walked right past the teacher's desk. Had she smelled
it?

He glanced up and saw her eyes move casually over him,
resting for half a second before moving on to his classmates. He
couldn't read her expression. Did she see the others looking at him?
He frowned at a girl nearby and shook his head. Couldn't they see
they were drawing attention to him?

The room was so quiet he could hear pages turn. A chair leg
scraped the floor. If he could just ask to go to the bathroom,
maybe he could ditch the shirt he was wearing and claim he'd
spilled something on it. He hoped the smell hadn't seeped into the
t-shirt he wore underneath. He shifted in his seat, trying to decide
if he should raise his hand from his desk. He couldn't risk going up
to the teacher. He held his breath as if holding his would keep her
from using hers.

Mrs. Addison stood up from her chair. He felt his hopes rise
as she headed toward the door. If she left the room for a minute,
he'd have time to figure out what to do. But then—she turned and
walked down the aisle, slowing at his seat. She crossed the back of
the room, walked toward the door, and picked up the telephone
from the wall.

"Could I have security?" she spoke clearly into the receiver. "I
need security up here right now." She glanced over at Courtney,
then looked away. Several of his classmates raised their eyebrows
at him. Rob winced. Courtney shrugged, slumped in his seat, and
looked down at his desk.

When the security guard arrived, she stepped outside to speak to him.

"Mr. Miles, we need you in the hall," she said, leaning back into the room. Someone near him said, "mmmm" to the tune of "shame" under his breath and everyone looked at Courtney. He got up and walked toward the door, heart pounding, fighting to breathe normally.

"What did I do?" he asked as she closed the classroom door. He wasn't about to admit guilt.

"You know what you did," she answered. "Mr. Miles has been smoking dope," she said to the guard.

"I ain't smoking dope," Courtney protested. "I don't do that stuff. You can ask anybody. They know I don't do drugs."

"I'm not stupid," she answered. "You think you can come up here smelling like marijuana and I'm not gonna know you've been smoking?"

"Let's go, Courtney," the guard said. "We can talk about this in the office."

"Look, I know you're not gonna believe me," he said, "but it was some people I rode to school with. I swear I never touched it."

"You're right, I don't believe you," she said, her parting shot as the guard ushered him down the hall.

"You can smell my hands," Courtney told the guard. "There's nothin' on 'em. Look at my eyes. I'm fine. I ain't been smoking."

In the principal's office he begged them to test him, but he was judged guilty without any further evidence. The teacher came down and spent several minutes talking to the principal behind a closed door. He later heard she'd insisted he get the maximum penalty allowed under school rules. The principal came out to deliver the verdict. He was expelled for the rest of the semester.

There was one factor that the school's administration did not take into consideration. His science teacher, the one who turned him in, was at that very moment embroiled in a lengthy divorce battle with Courtney's dad's cousin.

He walked home, dejected, to give his mom the news. He knew she'd be mad. And he knew she wouldn't help him argue his case. She rarely went to the school and would never have stood up to the authority figures there. She was probably right; everyone knows you can never win an argument against a teacher.

Sure enough, his mom whipped him for what seemed like a week, but the worst punishment was not being able to play basketball. Any time off from the game he loved was torture.

And now, because of Hurricane Katrina, his entire senior year of basketball was gone. How would he be eligible for college scholarships if he couldn't play high school basketball? Without a chance to play at a Division I school, his NBA dreams were over.

He knew he would suffer without Coach Moore's guidance also.

"You have a gift," he told Courtney. "It'll be taken from you if you don't use it. But you need to remember, everything's not just about basketball. You've got to work for your education too."

Coach Moore mixed his life lessons with his own brand of humor. When one of his players was slacking off, he'd point to the exit sign over the door, "See that sign? That's Latin for 'Get out the gym.' If you're not paying attention, and you don't wanna be here, you just go on out that door." No one ever left.

Courtney smiled at the thought of Coach Moore's efforts to keep him in line. They had gone nose to nose in a big playoff game last year. Courtney had put up some big numbers in spite of a case of pink eye. He'd gotten a little cocky halfway through the game and taken a crazy shot from half court, even though time was not running out. Coach Moore subbed him out, and Courtney was furious. Certain he'd say something from the bench that would get him in trouble, he left for the bathroom.

He tried to cool off before returning, but he was still angry when he came back. He plopped onto the bench and sat silent and fuming for what seemed like hours. As the game heated up, the crowd began to chant his name. He looked down at Coach Moore, but Coach stared straight ahead, refusing to acknowledge him. Finally, finally, he looked down at Courtney and said, "Ready?"

Courtney stood up. "What do you think? *I been* ready."

"You ain't ready. Sit down," Coach roared.

He left him there to work out his attitude. When he did allow Courtney back on the court, he played one of his best games ever.

Courtney's thoughts about Coach Moore made him even more depressed. He looked up at the hot sun outside Northside High and wondered how he was going to get a ride back to the trailer. And how was he going to tell Grandma Streets that he couldn't enroll in high school here? Maybe he could try another school, but transportation would be a problem since the bus that stopped at the FEMA trailer park came here.

A guy about his size coming out of the building eyed him curiously. "How ya doin'?" he said pleasantly.

"I'm okay," Courtney answered.

The boy was about to walk past him when Courtney stopped him. "Hey, I was just wondering, can you tell me what kinda basketball team y'all got at this school?"

"Well, I think it's pretty good—but that might be 'cause I play on the team. You play ball?"

"Yeah, I did, but my school closed after the hurricane, so I ain't playing now."

"Where're you from, man?" the boy asked him.

"L.B. Landry. Algiers."

"Y'all got a pretty good team, what I hear—mostly D-1 players."

"Yeah, well, we try."

"What's your name?"

"Courtney. Courtney Miles."

"Yeah, I think I read some stuff about you on the internet. Hey, why don't you come down tonight? It's open gym night starting at 5:00."

"Tonight? Man, that'd be great. I'm pretty outta shape. I ain't really played in a while, 'cept for shooting a few hoops."

"No problem. Just come on down and we'll see you get some playin' time."

Courtney forgot all about the woman in the office and her forms. His cloud of self-doubt lifted. What he needed was some time on the court.

playing bball at open gym

Chapter 15 – Get in Where You Fit In

"That's a great idea, Courtney. Maybe you'll feel better if you play a little ball," his grandmother told him as he left the trailer. She knew how unhappy he'd been, and she was worried. Several of his friends had called him about going back into the city, just to check things out. She had heard from others that Algiers wasn't safe right now.

Courtney caught a ride that night. The noises coming from the gym as he stood in the parking lot sounded like home. He opened the door, his pulse racing. He felt the adrenaline surge through his body as he entered the only environment that had ever made him feel he belonged.

He looked around the room, automatically checking out his competition. The gym was larger than Landry's, which had seemed small and homey with its white painted walls. There were about thirty people playing ball or watching. Courtney walked over near the water fountain to give himself time to get his bearings.

"All these guys play for Northside?" he asked a boy near the door.

"Most. A few come in for some five-on-five couple nights a week."

almost 30 people on their team

"Hey, you made it," he heard someone call in his direction. He looked up to see the same guy he'd talked to in front of the school. He thought he'd said his name was Keith, but he wasn't sure enough to use it. The boy was taller than he remembered, about 6'5", light skinned and muscular, like he worked out.

"How you doin'?" Courtney said, "Yeah, I 'preciate you tellin' me about open gym night."

"No problem. We 'bout to start it up."

"I just need to change clothes."

The boy pointed toward the locker room and Courtney headed off. When he came back, his new friend motioned him over and introduced him to the other guys who were playing.

"I ain't played much since the hurricane shut down my school. I need me a lil' workout if y'all can make some room for me." They made some room.

Courtney tried to ease into the game. He smiled to himself as he thought about trying to get in where you fit in, the same advice he'd given people fitting themselves onto his bus. He wanted to impress these guys he wasn't allowed to go to school with, but he didn't want to show his hand too early in the play.

He stretched upward, reaching high for a pass from a teammate who was eyeing him curiously. As he slid into an easy dribble, watching—without watching—for an opening to the goal, he felt his entire body relax. In the Cajundome he'd dreamed some nights that he was playing. Now, his entire world shrunk to the size of the court of the Northside High School gym.

All thoughts of storms and schools and floods and buses and police were gone. His concern for his grandmother...the ever-present worry over his mom...the fear of losing Jamie—it all receded into some remote storage space in his head. He knew nothing beyond the steady pulse of the dribble, the squeak of scuffling shoes on shiny hardwood, the feel of the raised pebbles as the ball flipped off his fingertips, the solid thunk on the backboard, and the soft swish of its passage through the net.

His body eased into the familiar patterns it craved – crouching, stretching, reaching. He launched off his toes, lifting into the air, floating above the court. For the first time in weeks he felt alive. Nothing else mattered but the game; it was impossible to hold back. The fast break, the pump fake, the easy lay-up, the hook shot—he scored again and again.

Courtney was aware of a long, low whistle from behind him as he sank a three-pointer from deep in the corner. His teammates stepped up their play to meet his challenge. Several people near the door stopped what they were doing to watch. He and his guys easily knocked off the competition, and they stopped for a rest break. As he wiped his head and neck with a towel, a stocky young guy, probably in his mid 30's, with short, dark hair approached him. Courtney had seen him watching from across the gym.

"Young man, what's your name?"

"Courtney Miles."

"Where'd you come from, Courtney?"

"L.B. Landry. Algiers."

"Coach Moore?"

"Ys, sir. He's my coach."

"Shame about your school. Y'all had a shot at the state championship before the storm came through."

"Yes, sir. We were gearing up for it."

"What kind of record you got at Landry?"

"I was averaging 17 points a game as a junior—with 8 rebounds."

"Pretty strong. Where are you living now?"

"I stay in a trailer with my Grandmama."

"One of the FEMA trailers?"

"Yes, sir, over off of Brothers Road."

"So you're a senior?"

"Uh-huh. I just started my senior year, um, when the storm came." Courtney was pretty sure he was still classified as a junior because of credits he hadn't earned, but it hardly seemed worth mentioning right now.

"Have you enrolled in school here yet?"

"No sir, I was trying to get in school here, but they told me I couldn't because my parents can't sign for me and my Grandma ain't my legal guardian."

The man rubbed his chin. "Let me see what I can do. Would you be interested in playing basketball for Northside?"

[handwritten: plays bball for Northside]

"Yes, sir. I'd be interested—real interested."

"You meet me in the office tomorrow morning and we'll see if there's anything we can do about the paperwork."

"Yes, sir. Thank you."

"7:45."

"I'll be there." [handwritten: coach got him in school]

Courtney was on time for once in his life and within minutes, he was enrolled. Obstacles like birth certificates and utility bills disappeared. No one seemed to care where his mama and daddy lived or who raised him or what piece of paper he had or didn't have. When his grandmother asked him the name of the man who had helped him, he was ashamed to tell her that he was so excited he forgot it. He never got to thank his mysterious admirer.

Once he started back to school at Northside, he made himself get up each morning, but it was tough to start over in a new place. His classes were crowded; the school was doing its best to absorb dozens of Katrina victims—the ones with parents to register them, Courtney assumed.

"The teachers, they're real nice," he told Jamie on the phone that night. "You can tell they're trying to help us 'cause they know we've been through a lot. But it's just not like being at home."

"You've got to study, Courtney," Jamie said. "If you get any further behind in school, it'll be hard for you to get into college."

"I know, but it's hard to focus with everything else going on and me trying to learn how to live in a whole new place. School just doesn't seem that important right now."

"Are there other people there from Landry?" she asked.

"Yeah, a few, but they're not in my classes. I'm in the middle of strangers all day. It's hard, you know, without my friends."

"Has anyone been able to go back home?"

"No, I talked to some people yesterday who went back to check on things, and they said everybody's stuff's gone. People came in after we left and took anything they could sell. I don't think there'll be anything left to go back to."

"So we'll just get new clothes and stuff when we get back, right? Everything'll be okay." *everything is gone in Algiers*

"Can't move back to a place that ain't got no power, Babe. Don't know if there'll ever be power and water again. They're saying they may not open up those neighborhoods again."

Jamie's silence made him feel bad for speaking so plainly. He knew it was even tougher for her – being so far away.

"Don't worry, Jamie. We'll figure something out. I'm not going to let anything split us up."

A small ray of hope came one night a few weeks after Courtney enrolled at Northside. He was sitting at the kitchen table in the FEMA trailer doing homework when his grandmother's cell phone rang. She answered and handed it to him.

"It's for you. It's Coach Ferguson." Charles Ferguson was assistant coach at Landry under Coach Moore and another of Courtney's mentors. Courtney reached eagerly for the phone. He'd heard from several former teammates that Coach had been able to place some of his former players in high schools near Algiers. He'd been working tirelessly to try to make sure his boys were all back in school.

"How's it going, Courtney?" Coach Ferguson asked.

Call from his old coach

168

"Pretty good." He hoped Coach would get to the point if he had news.

"And how's your grandmother?"

"She's good."

"Courtney, I wanted to see if you'd like to come back home to play ball. Helen Cox High School is reopening, and I've talked with Tyrone Mouzon, the coach over there, about you. Since Landry's not reopening, we might be able to get you in at Cox if you want to play there."

"I'd really like that, Coach. I'd like to come back." Helen Cox was in Harvey, near Gretna, which seemed closer to home that Courtney'd dreamed he could be. He stood up from the table grinning and began to pace the tiny room excitedly.

"You think you could find somewhere to live?"

"I've always found somewhere before."

"Well, let me get back in touch with you once I firm everything up. I'll call later in the week."

Courtney was ecstatic as he explained the plan to his grandmother. He was going home—well, almost. Even though Landry wouldn't reopen, he was sure some of his friends would register at Cox. Even having part of his old team back was a dream he'd given up on.

He promised Miz Gerry he'd find another player to live with, but in truth he planned to live alone. There were probably lots of empty houses now that Katrina had chased off so many West Bank residents. Electricity was not a necessity for him; he'd learned to live without it. And it had been hard for him to spend so much time with others over the past few months after so many weeks of living on his own, so he almost welcomed the isolation of his former living arrangement.

Courtney celebrated his good news by sleeping in the next day. In fact, he stayed home from school for the next two days. Why

169

should he spend more time at Northside if he was going back home?

But on the third day, Coach Ferguson called him back. He told Courtney he had bad news. He would not be able to get him on at Helen Cox. His academic eligibility was in question.

"I'm sorry, Courtney," he said. "It looks like I'm going to be able to get Maurice Foster back in school there, but I don't think we can work it out for you." Maurice was a friend of Courtney's, and it killed him to know he'd blown a chance at playing with Maurice at Cox because of his grades.

"I 'preciate you tryin' to help me, Coach," he told Ferguson on the phone, trying not to show how disappointed he was.

"I wish there was something I could do," Coach Ferguson told him.

"It's my fault. My absences are always keeping me down. I can do the work; it's not that it's too hard. It's just hard to make myself go to school when there's nobody saying I have to." He stopped and looked guiltily toward the bedroom where his grandmother had gone to try to give him some privacy. He hoped she didn't think he was blaming her. He blamed no one but himself for his problems with school.

"Courtney, you know this eligibility problem will probably keep you from playing at Northside too. I'm sure the coach there will be checking into it."

"Yes, sir." Courtney's heart sank.

"I'll keep my ear to the streets. If I find something else for you, I'll let you know."

Courtney hung up the phone and laid it on the table. He picked up a pencil and jabbed it into the paper he'd been writing. The lead broke and flew across the room.

"I'm sorry, Courtney," his grandmother said as she came back into the kitchen. She had heard enough to understand. "It was nice of Coach Ferguson to try to help you."

[handwritten margin note: Helen Cox didn't work out so he isn't moving back home]

Courtney got up from the table and walked back to his room without saying a word.

Several weeks later, he was stretched out on the bed in the trailer when he heard Grandma Streets' cell phone ring. She answered, came to his door, and handed the phone to him.

"Courtney, my name is Gil Dorsey-Wagner," said an unfamiliar deep voice. "I'm calling you from San Francisco. I got your number from Coach Ferguson. How you doin'?"

"I'm okay," Courtney said, wondering what this was about.

"I wanted to talk with you if you have a minute. Is this a good time?"

"Yes, sir, I can talk now."

"I've heard good things about you from Sweets Ferguson and also from Jamal Mundy. I'm calling to see if you might like to come out to California. Our school system has made some adjustments to the eligibility rules to allow Katrina victims start over out here in the Bay area. Would you be interested in going to school out here if we could arrange it?"

"I might be—if I know a lil' more about it." Jamal was a teammate at Landry, but Courtney had no idea how this man knew Jamal or Coach Ferguson.

"Well, I've got a place lined up where you could finish your senior year here in Oakland and play basketball—if you're interested. Would you like to play basketball again?"

"Yes, sir." Gil Dorsey-Wagner now had Courtney's full attention.

"The school is Castlemont High School, and you'd be playing for Gerald Pleasant. He's a great guy, very well respected, and a strong coach. We can find you a place to live out here and arrange for everything you need. How does that sound?"

"It sounds really good," Courtney was trying to process all this at once.

"And then if you do well in high school," Gil went on, "I can work on lining you up with a scholarship at one of the local junior colleges. I've been able to do that for a number of young men I've brought out here from all over the country."

"Yes, sir. Thank you." Courtney said. This all sounded too good to be true.

"There's just one thing, Courtney," Gil said. Courtney held his breath as he waited for the "catch," the condition that would make the entire idea impossible. Gil's tone became serious. "I understand that there are some grade issues. Coach Ferguson tells me that you're a smart guy, but your absentee problems have brought your grade point average down."

Courtney remained silent. He had no excuses to offer, so he waited to hear what Gil would say. "I've got to have your word that you'll study. School comes first to me. I want to help you get a good education and, if you get to play a sport you love, that's fine. But there has to be a commitment to improving your academic performance."

"Yes, sir, I understand. That's what I want, too—a good education."

"That's good to hear. If you want to continue to play ball at the college level, you have to get those grades up. Now, the school will help with tutors, but it'll be up to you to devote the hours needed to make up for the time you've lost, with the storm and all." Courtney wondered how much this man knew about his background—about the times he'd laid out of school, about his lackluster performance academically, about the failing grades that had resulted from his poor attendance record.

"Yes, sir, I'm gonna work real hard on my grades," he said now to Gil on the phone. "I know I've got to pull my GPA up if I want college coaches to look at me."

"Listen, you talk this over with your family, and give me a call back. If you decide you want to do this, we'll need to fly you out pretty soon so that you don't miss any more school."

"Yes, sir." Courtney was still too stunned to do much more than nod.

"I can send you a plane ticket and we can get you back in school within just a couple of days if you decide to come."

Courtney thanked Gil and hung up the phone. He turned to his grandmother who had been sitting at the kitchen table listening. He recapped Gil Dorsey-Wagner's proposal to her. "What do you think I should do?"

"It's a chance for you to go to school, Courtney. If Coach Ferguson knows this man and thinks he's okay, I think it might be the best thing for you to do right now."

She turned her head away, but not before he saw her eyes fill. California was so far away.

Courtney looked out the window of the trailer at the rows and rows of identical metal dwellings beside them. He walked closer to her and put his hands on her shoulders.

"What do you think, Courtney?" she asked quietly.

Courtney looked down at her, patted her on the head, and said. "I think you can't beat it with a bat." He picked up the phone and dialed Gil Dorsey-Wagner's number.

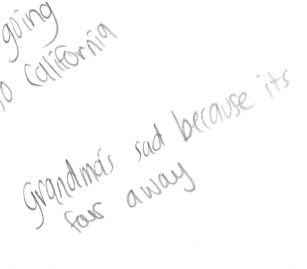

going to California

Grandma's sad because its far away

Chapter 16– Oakland

[handwritten: flying to California]

January 13, 2006. Courtney looked at the date on his boarding pass as the airplane taxied down the runway of the Lafayette/New Iberia Airport. One way. He was flying across the country to Oakland, California without any way to come home. He would be living 3,000 miles from his family, and he didn't know when he'd be back.

Day after tomorrow was Grandma Streets birthday. He would miss it. Hers was easy to remember—Martin Luther King's birthday. She always said his was easy to remember because it was on Flag Day, June 14.

[handwritten: 3000 miles away from family]

He'd tried to put on a cheerful face when he said goodbye this morning, but leaving home for the second time in just a few months was so hard. When he left Algiers on the bus after Katrina, he thought he'd be back in a few days. This time he knew it would be a long time. He leaned his head against the airplane window and closed his eyes as his vision blurred.

God, you know I'm gonna study hard and do my very best in my new school. But I don't know a single person there, and it won't be easy to live all the way across the country from my Grandmama and my friends. I've been by myself before, you know, lots of times, but I always felt like I was okay, long as

I was around the people I knew and the neighborhood I grew up in. This is gonna be real different for me. I need you to help me do good, and I'm asking you to take care of my Grandmama while I'm gone, and my mama and Jamie, too, and keep them safe until I come back."

Jamie was the first person he had called after talking to Gil that night.

"I think it's the best thing you could do, Courtney. If this man can help you get a college scholarship, you have to go."

"I just wish I could play ball and go to school somewhere closer to home."

"It might be good for you to be away from all this mess right now. Algiers is gonna be shut down for a while."

"It's just so hard to leave home – and you."

"I'll be here when you get back," Jamie said. "Don't worry, baby. Nothing's gonna change between you and me."

The shadow of the plane on the ground below him dimmed as they lifted into the air. Courtney watched the outline of the aircraft grow fainter until it finally disappeared. He worried that his former life would disappear, too, that his friends would forget him and his family would become accustomed to his absence. How would he visit with no money for the flight, and would he be able to come back home to see his mom when she got out of jail?

He slept for much of the trip to California. Several friends had come to see him off last night and they'd stayed up late, so he was tired. After he changed planes in Dallas, he shifted the small duffel bag that held all his earthly possessions under his seat to make room for his size 11 feet and slept again. He woke to a landscape that was brown, so different from the swampland of Louisiana. The barren desert hills below were dotted with sparse settlements connected by snaky roads along ridge tops. Then unexpectedly, vast sprawling neighborhoods appeared. In green valleys nestled between the brown hills, there were crowded cities—homes and buildings jotting every speck of land.

When he arrived in Oakland, he shouldered his carry-on bag, stretched his legs, and looked for the baggage claim exit where Gil had promised to meet him. He walked past throngs of people anxiously searching the moving carousels to the street outside. On the curb he watched for the silver, two-door Honda he'd been told to look for. He didn't have long to wait.

A trim, neat, fashionably dressed man pulled up, slid from behind the wheel of the car, and walked toward him, smiling. He was fortyish, friendly, and animated.

"Courtney?"

"Yes, sir."

"I knew it had to be you," he reached out to shake hands. "Welcome to Oakland. I'm Gil Dorsey-Wagner. How was your flight?"

"Great. Long, but it was good."

"Here, let's put your bag in the trunk," he said as he popped it open.

Courtney slid into the front seat and closed the door.

Gil's confident, down-to-earth manner put him at ease as they pulled into traffic while he talked. Instead of asking Courtney a lot of questions—which he had dreaded—Gil told him his own story.

Courtney was surprised at how much Gil's life had paralleled his own. He, too, had grown up with an absentee father, and a mother who spent many months in jail. Like Courtney, he lived on the streets. His own pathway to success, however, had detoured through a jail cell. He told Courtney that, because of a woman who claimed he'd done something he hadn't, he'd spent four years at Ryker's Island in New York City. Courtney knew the name of the famous prison from some of his favorite rap music.

"God wanted me to go to prison," Gil told Courtney. "Just like Paul, he changed me. He softened my heart and gave me a mission."

Courtney listened intently. This man was his sponsor, his chaperone, his temporary guardian. He wanted to know everything he could learn about him.

"During the four years I was in jail, I discovered I had a talent for working with young men, helping them get back their self respect. These were guys who'd lost their way; they didn't have any sense of self worth. I counseled with them and helped them get training for jobs while they were there. When they were released and they didn't return to prison, I felt my life was finally worth something."

Gil paused to see how Courtney was handling this new information. It was important for Courtney to trust him, but he wanted to be completely honest about his past.

"I decided to devote my life to helping guys who had no one else."

"Did you play basketball when you were in school?" Courtney asked.

"I've always loved basketball, but my father was the player. He and I reconnected after I was grown. He told me stories about playing ball for the Hawks in Milwaukee; that was before they moved to St. Louis and then Atlanta. But he got cut from the team in 1954 – he believed, for racial reasons. You've got to remember that when the team traveled, he wasn't allowed to eat in the same restaurants or sleep in the same motels as the other guys."

"I guess there weren't many black players then."

"Very few. I feel like the boys I've brought to the Bay area are his grandsons."

Gil paused and cleared his throat.

"Through me, in honor of him, you guys get a shot at playing pro. I want to give you boys a chance to be middle class. I want to give you a book and a basketball instead of a gun and a drug sack."

Courtney learned that Gil had spent months convincing the local junior college coaches that he was worthy of their trust. "I started in 2002 with four colleges offering one-year scholarships to boys from places like Harlem, Detroit, and New Orleans. I called some of the high school coaches I knew in those cities to match their players with opportunities here. After that I just kept networking and expanding. Now we've brought over fifty boys to high schools and colleges in the Bay area. That's fifty kids who'll have a chance to start life over away from the negative influences they were faced with in their own neighborhoods."

Gil told Courtney he'd be sleeping temporarily on his couch, that he was still working on living arrangements for him. He drove him to his small apartment, showed him where to keep his things, then took him out to meet his new coach, Gerald Pleasant. After they talked, Courtney knew Pleasant was a man who lived up to his name. He told his grandmother on the phone that night that Coach Pleas was not only kind, he felt he was a man he could trust to guide his game and his future.

After several days passed, Gil confessed to Courtney that he still hadn't found a family for him to live with. Courtney was worried he might have to return to Lafayette if something didn't work out soon. He was concerned that Gil had brought him out here without the living arrangements he'd promised, but how could he complain after all that he'd been given? He prayed that something would work out.

He tried to hide his nervousness on his first day at his new school. He nodded a friendly greeting to people in the halls who made eye contact, but kept to himself in most of his classes. It was not his style to push his way into already established cliques. To some extent, he liked life as an observer. He watched and listened, and his new environment gave him a chance to test his instincts about his classmates without knowing their history—instincts that were usually pretty good. He liked to trust people—until the point they proved untrustworthy. But he'd long ago learned that "Everybody who shakes your hand ain't your man," as he liked to

178

say. His Grandma had told him to "watch the quiet ones" and to stay away from people who want something from you.

Castlemont High was housed in a modern two-story building painted in bright coral colors.

The original school had originally started out in a medieval style structure, so the heraldry theme was still used—and overused.

The sports teams were the Knights and the school newspaper was Ye Castle Crier.

The yearbook was the Falcon and, of course, the student government association was the Round Table. Even though all of that seemed a little much, the idea of chivalry appealed to Courtney. The principles of courage, loyalty to your host, and reverence for God and country were ideals he'd based his life around.

Like the early knights, he also put women on a pedestal. His respect for the female gender was genuine, and his admiration of women took up much of his thinking time. He definitely enjoyed being surrounded by a new crop of girls, and he noticed several of them noticing him, but he stayed true to Jamie. He hated being so far away from her, but he wanted to become a man she'd be proud of.

He wanted to offer Jamie a better life, to be a good provider for the family they'd raise together. He knew she would wait for him. But he hadn't realized how tough it would be.

He called her every night, to tell her about a play he'd made in a game or a good grade on a math test, but sometimes it felt like their conversations trailed off in a way that made him anxious. He'd seen how hard it was for his mother to try to stay connected by phone from far away, and now he struggled with another long-distance relationship.

The first few weeks were hard. He missed his friends almost as much as he missed his girl. And then one night as he was making up his bed on the couch, Gil told him it would be his last night to sleep on it. He had good news. "I've found a place for you to stay. Coach Pleasant and his wife have agreed to take you in."

"You're serious? Man, that's really nice." Courtney was genuinely pleased. "Are you sure I won't be a bother to him? I don't want to intrude on his family after all he's done for me."

"It's fine. Coach Pleas has been impressed with your commitment to your school work and your ball team. He says they have an extra bedroom you can use until we work out something more permanent."

Coach Pleas picked him up in his Jeep the next day, and Courtney realized as they pulled up in front of the small, attractive house on the corner lot, that he'd already known what it would look like. Like the man, the house was pleasant—neat and friendly and clean. The white wood, brown trim, and black iron-fenced yard were immaculate. Mrs. Pleas was at the door, waiting with a smile for her new boarder. She showed Courtney to his own room downstairs, treating him more like visiting royalty than a homeless boy from Louisiana.

He sat on the cheerful bright blue and red blanket and took in his new surroundings. He smiled as he picked up the matching blue pillow and noticed his own small TV on the bedside table. That night he talked easily with his new family at dinner in a home that seemed to him to be "just-moved-in" fresh. Coach Pleas, who often did the cooking, made teriyaki chicken with rice and yams.

"Coach Pleas and his wife, they just took me in with arms wide open," he told his grandmother on the phone. "Their son, Gregory—he's five—he's a great kid, and he's always asking me to play pitch and catch with him outside."

"Are you helping with the chores?" Grandma Streets wanted to know.

"Yes, ma'am. I help with dishes, and I told Coach I could cut the grass."

"Are you working hard in school?"

"Yes, ma'am. Coach makes sure I do my homework, and all my teachers have been helping me out. It's pretty hard, but I've been in study hall every day."

"I want to see that report card. I still haven't seen any grades."

"Don't worry, Grandmama. I know I have to stay on top of my work. It took me a lil' minute to figure it out, but I know now it's in my own hands. I'm gonna work for my dream."

Neither of them ever mentioned the terrible thing he'd done to her last summer, a few months before the storm came through. He still burned with shame when he thought of it.

Miz Geraldine had learned he wouldn't be enrolled in senior level classes unless he made up two credits for classes he failed, so she took the little money she had, went down to the school, and paid for summer school. All summer, she left the house for work each day thinking he was going to school, but he just didn't go. She spent her small savings to help him finish high school, and he wasted her money.

He still cringed with the guilt at the memory of the look on her face when he finally confessed what he'd done. Her quiet disappointment was more devastating than any punishment she could have handed out. He had betrayed her faith in him, abused her trust, and squandered her hard-earned money. It was a mistake that would haunt him for years to come.

It wasn't that he was lazy. It was just hard for him to admit how far behind he had fallen during all the months he skipped so many days of school. He knew he was digging the hole even deeper, but he worried that the gap was too wide to close. He was afraid of failure. He was afraid he couldn't do the work.

He was determined to make it up to her now. "I've never been this focused before," Courtney told his grandmother now. "There's nothing that can distract me. I plan to roll with this chance I've been given."

"You can do anything you set your mind to if you work hard enough," she told him. "Are you happy there, Courtney?" she asked.

"I am. Oakland's got a very cool vibe," he told her. "It's a lot like New Orleans 'cause there's so many people from all over." Courtney described for her how International Boulevard flowed from one ethnic neighborhood to another. One minute you were walking past taquerias with names like El Pollo Loco and the Latino market with its painted murals and bright banners. Then the scenery changed to the New Saigon Supermarket and signs advertising Vietnamese Beef Noodle soup and Cambodian Chinese fast food.

He liked the way Oakland's businesses reflected the city's racial mix—Amigo Realty, Ebony Beauty salon, and Kung Fu Academy. In front of a place called Fresh Out the Barber Shop, a sign said, "Braid It or Fade It." Liquor stores and pawn shops coexisted peaceably with adult learning programs and summer youth centers. The street vendors at Fruitvale and the open markets reminded him of the French Quarter with its earthy smells—sometimes appetizing, sometimes overripe and rank.

He felt better after he began to learn the names of his classmates. His new ball team gave him a built-in family that helped make things easier.

"Have you made a lot of new friends?" Jamie asked him.

"Yeah, some," he answered. "People always want to ask me questions about driving the bus—after that article came out."

Courtney had agreed to tell his story when an Oakland Tribune reporter called him for an interview. Enough time had passed that he felt he could come clean about his role in the post-Katrina rescue. He still didn't like to talk about it. Praise made him uncomfortable, and he didn't want students at his new school to make judgments—good or bad—about his stealing a bus.

"I don't like it when people say 'Renegade Bus' because it sounds like I did wrong. And I don't like it when they use the word 'hero' either."

"But you are a hero," Jamie laughed.

"No, I'm just a regular guy who was given an opportunity by God to help people I loved. If there was anything special about that, it was the great blessing I was chosen to receive."

"Well, you're my hero, anyway," she said. She couldn't see the huge smile that brought to his face on the other end of the phone. That was a role he was happy to accept. "You just be careful around all those California girls," she told him more than once.

Courtney met people fairly easily, but he was shy around girls. He felt he'd spent so much time with guys on the basketball court, he forgot how to act when females were a part of the crowd. After he played his first two games at Castlemont and Coach Pleas moved him to a starting position in the third game, he was aware of a definite increase in the attention he received from the school's female population. He had shown off a little in the third game, once he had become more confident and relaxed, and the girls took notice.

He didn't like to brag, but he'd been told he was handsome, and his easy-going personality had often charmed the ladies in the past. But his attentions to the Castlemont girls remained limited – by the time constraints of his practices and by his continuing loyalty to Jamie. At night he lay in bed and envisioned her face. He sometimes had a panicked feeling that he'd forget what she looked like. And he tried not to think about what would happen if she forgot him.

And then something amazing happened.

Someone else read the articles about him in the newspaper— someone outside the student body of his new high school.

Someone who cared a great deal about Courtney Miles' accomplishments.

Only a couple of months had passed since Courtney had come to Castlemont. He was sitting in class finishing an assignment when a voice on the intercom summoned him to come to the front office. He looked up at the teacher in surprise. Had he done something wrong?

As he entered the office, he saw a tall older man standing near the counter with the counselor. The man looked up and smiled. Courtney froze and stared back in confusion. The man looked just like him!

"Courtney, do you know who I am?" the man asked.

"Yes," Courtney answered without any hesitation. "You're my grandfather."

"How did you know that?" Gerald Ruffin asked him. "I haven't seen you since you were really young."

"I just knew," Courtney answered, his heart pounding.

"Did you know I was living in Oakland?"

"No, I woulda looked for you if I did," he told his grandfather. "I knew you were in California, but my Grandma said she didn't know what city. How did you know I was here?" he asked.

"I opened my newspaper yesterday and there you were. I couldn't believe it when I saw the article. I looked to see if it gave your address, and that's when I saw you were at Castlemont. So I called the school and asked them if I could come and reintroduce myself. They asked me a lot of questions and then they said I could come and meet with you in the office."

"You live near here?"

"Just right up the road."

"That's hard to believe, that I would come out here to live and be just a 'lil ways from where you've been living."

"It's just a short ride on the BART train. Do you think maybe you could come for a visit on Saturday?"

"Yes, sir, I'd like that."

Miz Geraldine was amazed when he told that night about meeting his grandfather. She hadn't known for several years where her former husband was living.

"How did you know who he was?" she asked him on the phone.

"I just had this feeling. He was looking at me with eyes that looked like mine."

"You're right, you and Gerald do have the same eyes. You have your Dad's nose, but you've got your grandfather's eyes."

"I remember those old pictures you had of him, but I ain't seen him since I was, what—seven or eight, so it wasn't like I recognized him. I just knew. It's crazy; the chances of me coming to live in the same town as him are about like the chances of me driving that bus right to where you were at the Cajundome. God works in mysterious ways."

That Saturday Coach Pleasant dropped Courtney at the BART station and his grandfather met him at the Coliseum stop just a few stops away. They chatted easily on the five minute ride to his house on Weld Street.

"That's it, just ahead," Gerald nodded as they pulled over to allow another car to pass on the narrow, single lane road. He pulled up to the wooden shotgun house painted light green, unlocked the door, and stepped aside for Courtney to bring his bag into the small but comfortable living room.

"I hope you don't mind sleeping on the couch," he said.

"The couch'll be just fine," Courtney told him.

They spent that night getting reacquainted and establishing a tradition that would become a favorite pastime for the two of them – watching cowboy movies on television. Courtney didn't mind at all that there wasn't quite enough sofa for his long legs; he was spending time with his Grandpa.

A few weeks later, he had more news for his grandmother. "Grandpa asked me if I want to move in with him. I've been going out there a couple of times a week, and he told me I can just stay out there."

"That's really good of him, Courtney. Is that what you want to do?"

"It's a little ways out for me, but I can take the BART in to school. As much as I love Coach Pleas' house, I can't stay with them forever. They've been real nice, but I don't want to be a burden to them, and now that I have family here, it's where I belong."

"It's your decision," his grandmother said.

"I want to spend time with my Grandpa. We're going fishing next weekend in Stockton. It's not too far away."

Courtney hung up the phone, opened his biology book, and stared blankly at the page. He had painted rosy pictures for his grandmother about his classes and his grades, but the truth was, his first few months in school had been really tough academically. He forced himself to listen in class, but half the time he barely knew what was going on. No matter how hard he tried to stay connected to the lecture, the teacher's voice would fade into the background as his thoughts wandered.

He knew his chronic absences had left gaping holes in his knowledge. There was nothing sequential about the way he'd learned math. To compensate, he would second guess himself, scrubbing out answers with his eraser in frustration, answers that often were right. He didn't want anyone to know how slowly he read, and writing assignments took hours to complete.

He was not one to ask for help, but he was becoming more and more worried about living up to his goals. The school counselor had already told him he wouldn't be able to graduate with his class because of lost credits. It was upsetting news, but she assured him he could enroll at one of the community colleges without a high school degree—if he passed the exit exam. For Courtney it was a big if.

Gil had promised to talk with the local junior college coaches about him, but there would be no talks and there would be no scholarship without a passing score on the exit exam. His entire future rested on one test—and he was terrified.

Help came from an unexpected source when an English teacher named Vicki Stoneham stopped him in the hall one day. Vicki was not his teacher, but he knew who she was. She was known as the teacher a lot of kids trusted and turned to for help. He had said hello to her in the hall a couple of times as they passed, but they'd never had a conversation.

"So, Courtney, how are you doing?" she asked him, fixing him with her intense gaze.

"I'm ah'right," Courtney said, his cocky tone contradicted by something in his eyes. She continued to look directly into his face. He looked away from her and down at his feet.

"I want to know the truth," she said in her no-nonsense tone. "Some of the other students told me you're having a hard time. Your friends are worried about you."

"Well, I've got to be honest with you," he admitted, unable to keep up the pretense any longer, "Things aren't too good right now."

"Come in and sit down. I want you to tell me what's going on in each class. I think I can help you."

Vicki set up a meeting of all of Courtney's teachers. She made sure they understood his situation—that he had missed an entire semester of school because of Katrina. Added to the absences he'd racked up while scrounging for food alone in an abandoned house for half of his junior year, much academic damage had been done. She reminded his teachers how hard it must have been for him to attend classes and study when he didn't have enough to eat and was trying to sleep in a house without power or water for months at a time. She asked for extra patience, and she asked them to contact her about any specific problems they were seeing so that she could help him.

Once they understood how hard he was trying to overcome the deficits caused by the chaos in his life, his teachers paid more attention to him in class and spent more time with him after school. The cocky attitude he'd adopted in class as a defense against his terrible insecurity had convinced them he just didn't care about his grades. Nothing could be further from the truth. When they were made aware of his situation, they began to look for ways to help him catch up.

Because of the Oakland school system's low academic performance, it had received a grant from the Bill & Melinda Gates Foundation fund set up to revitalize failing schools, so Vicki and his teachers helped him make use of all the resources available to him—from remediation programs on computer to tutors. His grades began to improve. The panic he'd felt sitting in classes he couldn't comprehend began to dissipate as the subjects he studied came into focus. Vicki's willingness to step in as a counselor helped him turn things around academically.

When he was most frustrated with school, those were his times to shine on the basketball court. It was his proving ground, and a strong performance always boosted his self esteem. During his games, he caught himself looking for Jamie—on the sidelines where she always sat, wearing his number. Fresh grief washed over him each time he realized she wasn't there, and his loneliness was a palpable pain.

He talked to his grandmother most every night. She insisted he call after practices even though the time difference meant it was two hours later for her. "Boy, you'd better not call me before 9:00," she would tell him if he forgot and called earlier—before the rates went down.

"I've got to behave or you'll take me off your Favorite Five," he kidded her.

"Now, you know that'll never happen," she said. He was pretty sure he was Number One on her Favorites list.

"I've been working hard on my playing skills. Not to put stars on my head or anything, but I had a 'lil part in the city championship," he told her. "And the section tournament title, too."

"You been going to church every Sunday?" she asked.

"Yes, ma'am. I really like Beebe Memorial. I'm glad Teedy and Don asked me to start going with them." Vicki and Don Stoneham had become Courtney's Oakland family. He called her "Teedy", his nickname for Auntie, and she called him "Nephew." Their church adopted Courtney and became his extended family, the West coast version of his Fischer projects family in Algiers.

And then it happened—something that was just short of miraculous in his mind. He received word that he'd passed the exit exam!

He ran to Vicki's room to tell her the news. He knew she'd be as excited as he was. He wasn't sure there was anything he'd ever done that made him feel prouder. He couldn't wait to call his grandmother that night.

He felt he'd redeemed himself for the academic failures he'd racked up during high school. He was finally on the right road to a strong education. Hurricane Katrina would not keep him from realizing his dreams.

And then there was more good news.

"I've set up a meeting for you next week with Justin Labagh," Coach Pleasant told him. "He's the basketball coach at City College of San Francisco. Gil and I talked with him about you, and he wants you to come down to discuss your game and your academic

got a scholarship

record." Courtney hoped they'd spend more time talking about his game than his grades.

The day they met with him, Courtney liked Coach Labagh and the City College campus.

"We can offer you a scholarship to pay for classes and books, but you'll be on your own for room and board," Coach LaBagh told him.

"I really like what I've seen," Courtney said. "I'd like to go to school here, but I'm afraid transportation might be a problem. I'll be living with my grandfather in Oakland, and it's about thirty minutes away. I'm not sure I can afford the subway every day."

"Let me look into that," Coach Labagh said and left the room for a few minutes. He came back with a smile.

"Coach Tom, one of my assistants, lives near where you'll be, and he's agreed to pick you up every day." Courtney was overwhelmed with the many kindnesses that had been shown to him during his time in California.

Coach Tom take him to school

He was also worried about food, clothing, and other expenses. Practices would keep him from having time for a job, even a partime one. He didn't want to depend on his grandfather's limited income to support him. He had come out here on his own, and he knew he would find a way to make it on his own.

As the end of the school year approached, Vicki called him in to her room again. Coach Pleasant had told her that the City College scholarship didn't pay for room and board. "As long as you continue to do well in school," she told him, "I have a place where you can stay. It's an apartment my family owns. It's small, but you can live there on your own while you go to college."

Courtney couldn't believe how generous everyone had been with him. He felt humbled, and he made up his mind to pay them back by working hard to show he was worthy of their trust.

He moved into the apartment on 40th Street a few weeks later. As much as he loved spending time with his Grandpa, he knew

moved into Vicki's apartment close to his college

he'd study more in the quiet apartment. Now he felt truly independent.

He was going to college—a life-long dream fulfilled. Everything had come together in a way he could never have foreseen. He knew he could succeed, and he was determined to prove himself.

his dreams came true

Chapter 17 – A College Education

Life in the big city was a huge change.

"This is the best time of my life so far. I've seen things I ain't nevah seen before," Courtney told his grandmother, his soft Louisiana accent full of wonder. "San Francisco is huge, and the campus is really big, too. I was tardy to class twice last week because I couldn't find where I was going. I just got lost."

"You like your teachers?" Miz Gerry asked.

"Yes ma'am, I've got me a good schedule, and it's nice not to go to the same classes every day. There's nobody ringing bells to tell you where to go, or making you ask to go to the bathroom." High school rules had always seemed unnecessarily rigid to someone used to making all his own decisions. It was one reason he stayed away so much.

"Are you keeping on top of your school work?"

"Yes, ma'am, they make us go to study hall, so I know I'll get my work done."

Courtney worried that he wasn't getting much playing time at first. "Coach Justin, he's great. I just got to prove myself to him. I'm gonna show him what I can do," he said. "And I'm getting along real good with the other guys on the team. Today I worked with a guy on his dribbling. At first he couldn't get it for nothin', and finally it clicked with him. First behind the back, half court— cross over, base line—cross over. You do it fifteen times and you've got it."

He had settled into a familiar routine at his new school: his favorite pre-game snack—Skittles, and his favorite practice gear— black tights. He liked the way tights kept his muscles warm and loose, and the coach let him wear them during games unless they were wearing white uniforms.

He told his grandmother his coaches were extra hard on him, but he knew they were on him for his own good. "The coach ain't giving me any favors when I'm scoring big in a game. He's gonna call carrying, traveling, charging— I don't get away with anything."

"That's good they're making you work. It means they feel you have potential."

"I been meaning to tell you, my Dad's been calling me a lot since I been out here," he told Miz Gerry. "He calls me to talk about which college coaches have shown an interest in me and what schools I should consider." Courtney wasn't sure why Damon Williams had begun to take more of an interest in his life these days. It felt strange, after all the years he spent with just his grandmother and mother, to have the guidance of three adult men – his grandfather, Don Statham, and now his dad.

"You know he never played much, but he always has lots of advice, mostly about attitude and commitment on the court." Such advice seemed a little ironic to Courtney from a man who hadn't shown much commitment to his son for most of his life. But he knew that his dad was making an effort now, so he tried to be patient with his input.

"You've got to be open to different types of college programs," his Dad told him.

"Don't worry," Courtney said. "I'll go wherever they want me. I'm on my knees every night asking God to show me where I'm supposed to be."

"Are you working on that transcript and studying for the ACT?"

"Yes, sir." He knew he had to score at least a 17 for NCAA qualifying standards.

"You just do your best, son. That's all anybody's asking."

He tried to tell himself that his dad, for the most part, had done his best, too. Like so many men he'd known in the projects, Damon had made mistakes when he was young—mistakes that later kept him from finding decent jobs that would pay the bills.

He figured it must have been hard on his father to watch his mother sell drugs to provide for her son what he couldn't afford to give him. Maybe it was easier for his dad to walk away than to admit he wasn't able support his family financially—easier to pretend he *wouldn't* than to admit he *couldn't*. With money worries of his own, Courtney was better able to understand how financial problems had played into his dad's absence from his life.

In the Fischer projects, lots of young people escaped the frustrations of poverty with drugs; the high of cocaine was fast and easy to come by. From using to selling wasn't a huge leap. Selling crack was easy money. It was hard to settle for a job flipping burgers when making good choices didn't always feed your family. And once they were picked up by the police, even on possession charges, even for non-violent offenses, they were never able to find jobs again.

His father had never made a commitment to his mother, either, but Courtney felt he now understood a little better his dad's reluctance to get married. A lot of the guys he knew in their teens and early twenties didn't want to commit to a future because they didn't really believe they'd have one. Watching so many friends die as homicide victims made Courtney appreciate every new day he

194

was given. He wanted to make plans that included a commitment to Jamie.

"I want to give my dad a chance to be part of my life now," he told Jamie on the phone. "Even though he wasn't really around much for all those years, there were times when he tried to make it up to me—like that one Christmas he invited me to stay with him and his family 'cause my Mom was in jail."

He didn't see his half-siblings enough to feel he knew them, but he knew his dad was trying. His father had wrapped packages for him and tried to make it a good holiday for Courtney. But gifts meant nothing when his mother was locked up. If he could have wrapped just an hour with her in shiny paper, that would have been the best present he could ever have.

"I think he really wants to help out, now that he's settled down and straightened out his life. He's doing a good thing, helping a lot of kids stay straight." Damon and his family lived at Hope Haven, an orphanage that had been turned into a residential home for abused, neglected, and delinquent youth, where he was a foster father/social worker.

Courtney was proud of his dad's work with high school dropouts and at-risk kids—although he'd never understood the term "at risk." Had his dad ever considered him "at risk"—at risk of not having a dad...at risk of having nowhere to stay...at risk of having nothing to eat. How "at risk" did he have to be to get his father's attention?

When anger over his long absence resurfaced, he pushed it aside. His dad seemed genuinely interested in what was going on in Courtney's life in Oakland, and his conversations with him helped him stay connected to his home in Louisiana. Damon even sent him a little money sometimes when he needed help.

Money was a constant source of stress. When he ran out of food or had to pay his utility bill, he called on his family. Different relatives would send him what they could, but none of them had much beyond what it took to live day-to-day.

On his forearm was a cartoon Tasmanian devil tattoo with a duffel bag below it and the words "Duffel Bag Boy." "I was really young when I had it done," he told Jamie when she first asked him about it. "I'm thinking about having it removed. It seems silly now, but it represented a goal that was important to me. I wanted to have enough cash to take care of my Grandmama, my mom, and my dad. I wanted to have enough to buy nice presents for them and to never have to worry again about where we were gonna get food or where we would sleep. I wanted a duffel bag full of money."

Only once had the need for money driven him to desperation—the day he found a plastic bag of marijuana in an alley. He was twelve at the time, his mom was back in jail, and he and his grandmother were living day-to-day on her small salary, sometimes going to bed hungry when there wasn't enough food. He was walking by himself through the project and saw the small sandwich bag in the shadows where someone had tossed it, either by accident or while running from the cops. Without even opening it, he knew what it was, but a quick whiff of the contents widened his eyes in confirmation.

It seemed so easy—to take advantage of an opportunity that had landed literally at his feet. In just a few minutes he could have enough money for them to eat on for a week or more. He looked around to make sure no one saw him, picked up the bag, and stuck it in his pocket. Nervous but determined, he walked down to the corner where he knew he'd find guys who'd be interested. His hand shook a little as pulled the bag out to show them.

"I've got something I think you might want," he said as he approached the man he knew best. He shifted from one foot to the other, searching for the right words to strike the deal.

His life of crime ended abruptly when his would-be buyer snatched the bag from his hand, smacked him on the back of the head, and said, "What the hell you think you're doing, son? You know better than to get in the middle of some shit like that. Give me that."

When he prayed, he never prayed for material things. He figured God had more important things to do. But he wondered if he'd ever reach the point where he didn't struggle to survive. His life was a constant barrage of financial problems—trying to get the power turned back on before the little food he had in the refrigerator went bad, borrowing cell phones from friends to call his grandmother so she wouldn't worry, calling his relatives when he ran out of money for food, and scrounging enough money for the bus or subway when he needed to get to class. His dream of playing in the NBA kept him focused. He wanted nothing more in life than to make a solid living playing basketball so he could make a home with Jamie.

Courtney worked hard at City College. Now that he knew he could do the work academically, he could concentrate on honing the basketball skills that would allow him to play for one of the big colleges after he finished junior college. He felt his life was finally moving in the right direction.

And then he got some devastating news about Jamie.

Working hard at College

Did Jamie find someone else?

Chapter 18 – Alone Again

[handwritten: talks to his mom]

[handwritten margin: Jamie might be cheating on him]

There had to be some mistake. Courtney hung up his cell phone and stared at the wall. He was sure this was a misunderstanding. His mother had just told him, in one of his rare phone conversations with her, that a friend of hers from Algiers had seen Jamie coming out of the grocery store with another guy.

"Courtney," Gabriel said, "I don't want to be the one to tell you, but you have to know. Jamie's cheating on you."

She was wrong; that was all there was to it. People went to the grocery store together all the time. He and Jamie both had friends of the opposite sex. It had never been an issue. Jamie knew there was no one else for him, and he was sure she felt the same way.

Didn't she?

Courtney picked up his phone and dialed Jamie's number. She would straighten this out. When she answered, he tried to speak calmly – no sense pouncing on her with accusations over what was probably an innocent friendship.

"Jamie, I need you to be straight with me," he finally said. "Somebody I know saw you coming out of the grocery store with a guy. Who was it you were with?"

Silence. There was no answer.

"Jamie, talk to me. I need to know what's going on."

Jamie started to cry.

198

Courtney's legs turn to jelly. He felt a buzzing in his head, and he reached for a chair.

There was more, and the news tore Courtney's world apart.

Jamie— his Jamie —was pregnant.

She was carrying another man's child.

"I wanted to tell you, but I just didn't know how," she said, sobbing. "I picked up the phone to call you so many times, and I just couldn't do it. I didn't know how to say the words."

Courtney wished she could take them back—the words that had shattered all his hopes.

He listened for as long as he could without speaking, then he dropped the phone. He heard her voice calling to him as he sat with his head in his hands, rocking back and forth.

This wasn't happening. She had promised to wait for him.

She said nothing would ever keep them apart.

She said he was the one she wanted to spend the rest of her life with.

She said she loved him.

She said…she said…she said. But what she *did* was something else.

He picked up the phone and turned it off, then went outside. He walked for hours without really knowing where he was. How could she disrespect everything they had together? She knew he was doing what he had to do to get an education. She knew he would be with her every minute if he could. How could she give up on him like this?

So many times he'd been tempted to go out with other girls out here in California, but he walked away. He had spent his time alone to honor his promise to Jamie. He walked the dark streets for hours that night, asking himself what he might have done differently, trying to figure out where it had all gone wrong.

Later, in the small hours before dawn, he called her back. They talked for over an hour. He never revealed to anyone what

they said—the private conversation that took place on the worst
night of his life. To his friends he said only that things were over
between them, but that he still thought Jamie was a good person.
She was real with him, talked to him honestly about the way she
felt about him and how hard it had been while he was away. He
knew the baby's father but was not friends with him.

Jamie had grown up like he had, without a father. A lot of the
girls he knew did crazy things to get the attention of a guy. So
many of them just wanted a man in their lives—and a baby to love.
Some girls who had never had anything thought of a baby as a
possession - the one thing that belonged to them that no one could
take away. The one person who would love them unconditionally
forever. It was a selfish viewpoint, he understood that, but he also
knew how hard it was to be alone.

For days Courtney obsessed about his loss. He replayed
conversations in his head, looking for clues he might have seen.
How had he been so wrapped up in his own life that he missed the
disconnect Jamie was feeling?

Had he made the wrong decision, leaving her thousands of
miles away to come to school out here? Could anyone's love
survive that kind of distance and time apart? Maybe he'd been
dreaming to think it could ever work out.

Courtney survived the next few weeks by throwing himself
into school and basketball. His concentration was off, but he was
determined to make up for it with sheer sweat and drive. He
pushed himself on the court and off, blocking thoughts of Jamie
when they threatened to mess with his head.

Everything he'd thought about his future had been turned
upside down. He could not imagine life without Jamie. Even with
all the problems he'd faced throughout the tough years of his life,
he'd never known just getting out of bed in the morning could be
so hard. But he had to find a way to put one foot in front of the

other—to keep going even on days when he didn't feel like doing anything

After a few months at City College, Don called him to talk with him about an idea he'd had. "Vicki and I want you to consider changing schools. The commute into San Francisco is eating up a lot of your study time. Myron Jordan is a friend of ours, and he's the coach at the College of Alameda. It's only five minutes away." As much as Courtney liked Coach LaBagh, the move to a new school made sense to him.

Maybe a change would help him clear his head and get a new start without Jamie. At the end of his freshman year, he left City College to enroll at Alameda.

Coach Jordan met with him to review his records. He'd worked hard on his grades at City College, but it made sense to redshirt him for his first year at Alameda. Suspending his eligibility for one year would give him more time to pull up his GPA. He would attend classes and practice with the team, but he would not play in the games.

"It's hard to sit out the games, "he told his grandmother, "but my mindframe is thinking about the future."

Being redshirted didn't stop Courtney from moving into a leadership role on his team, organizing practice sessions and helping coach teammates with specific needs. He had always loved studying the dynamics of a team, quickly learning which players favored a fast pass and who wanted a bounce pass in certain situations. He was sometimes hard on his teammates, berating them when they missed easy shots.

"Just tell them once," Coach Jordan told him. "You make your point with them, then move on. Don't beat a dead horse. They'll learn from their mistakes, just like you do."

But he was equally hard on himself, isolating his own problem areas and working to correct them. He practiced his left-hand dribble for hours, working to strengthen the wrist that had given him trouble since childhood.

"Alameda's closer than City College, so I catch the bus to school," he told his grandmother. "That gives me more time to study. Coach Jordan taught me how to handle my business on the front end so I don't have to rush at the end. Once I made up my mind to study first, I found out I had a lot more time for other stuff. I've learned to finish what I *need* to do before doing what I *want* to do." His proudest moment was the day he told her he was making B's now.

When he was lonely, Courtney played one of his mother's CD's he'd brought from home. Most of the time he listened to his own music—hip-hop or rap, but when he played his mom's old R&B songs, he could picture her dancing around the house singing. He tried to substitute his memories of her in happier times for the memory of the last time he'd visited her in St. Gabriel, down below Baton Rouge, dressed in an orange prison uniform and sitting in the cold, impersonal family visitation room on a metal folding chair.

One of her favorite singers was Kelly Price. He sat down on the couch and stared vacantly at the wall while he listened to the lyrics of "Love Sets You Free." The line about facing a hurricane seemed written just for him. He had faced the hurricane. He had braved the darkness. And now he had lost the love he thought could set him free.

He wished he knew where this chapter in his journey would end. He knew he'd broken the shackles of apathy—the bonds of his own lack of commitment that had held him back in school. But his sunshine, his Jamie, was gone.

There were nights when he lay in bed in the darkness thinking about her. What good was his success—in school and in basketball —without someone to share it? He'd been alone for most of his life, but since ninth grade, he'd always believed he'd have Jamie.

202

She had been his "Bay," short for baby. When he surprised her with small bouquets of roses from the grocery store, he always promised her that one day he'd buy her "one thousand roses—plus one more". It was just a little joke between them, something he always said to her. He loved the smile it brought to her face.

thinks about Jamie a lot

He did believe that love could set you free. He knew his grandmother loved him, his mother loved him, but would it be enough to keep him moving forward? It would be hard to find the strength to keep fighting for what he wanted without Jamie.

He went to movies by himself and sat in the dark. It had always been the only way he could forget his problems for an hour or two. But the closing credits brought him back to reality, and he walked home alone. Sometimes he soaked in the bubble baths he'd loved all his life. It was a guilty pleasure he didn't advertise for fear of ruining his tough guy image on the team, but it was one of the few antidotes he'd found for insomnia. He'd relax in the tub until his eyelids grew heavy, then dry off, powder himself up, and curl his long limbs, still warm from the hot soapy water, into sleep.

friends are moving closer to him because of Gil

One morning Gil Dorsey-Wagner called him with an unexpected surprise. His cousin Rob Wallace and his friends Reginald Ruffin and Kelvin Hodges would be flying out at the end of the week to enroll at Las Positas, a junior college in Livermore, just a few miles away. Courtney had told Gil about his friends back home who played ball with him at Landry. Gil had provided local coaches with information about them and worked to find scholarships for them in Oakland. Like Courtney, they would play basketball, study to improve grades, and hope to get picked up by coaches from schools like Georgetown, UCLA, and others.

Having friends close by who shared a common history was a huge morale boost for Courtney. He had heard Louis Armstrong sing "Do you know what it means to miss New Orleans?" Courtney ached for a small taste of home. When his friends arrived in Oakland, he spent their first weekend with them, and it was the first time he'd laughed out loud in weeks.

They stayed up late the first night he saw them, catching up on the past months. They spoke in the shorthand of people who've known each other a lifetime, half-finishing inside jokes before getting cut off by someone else.

Brutally honest and always making fun of each other, they made a game out of pointing, without a word, to the person who said something dumb or came in with a comment too late. They ganged up on the victim until everyone was unanimous in silently calling them out.

Reginald stood up to act out a tale he was telling. He moved around the room, nudging his friends to make sure they were paying proper attention, an unnecessary precaution because when Reginald told a story, everyone listened.

"So, Streets, we decided to go back to Algiers; it was just a few weeks after you left. Our parents didn't want us to, but we had to see for ourselves if our stuff was still there."

"Was it?" Courtney interrupted.

"Nah, man. It was gone. Everything we had. Somebody went in and cleaned us out."

"Yeah, that's what I thought." Courtney knew the things he left at Fischer the day he drove the bus out of Algiers had probably all been stolen, too, in his long absence.

"So, listen," Reginald continued with his story, "Man, it was creepy there, you know, with no power on or nothin'. All five of us ended up all sleeping in one room 'cause we was scared. No, come on, don't lie," he said, reacting to Rob's facial expression. "You know it's the truth, Rob." He turned back to Courtney. "Rob tried to sleep in the living room, but he came back there with us too."

"So there's like no power and everything's dark and real, real quiet."

204

"You could hear glass break out in the street," Rob broke in.

"You tellin' this story or me?" Reginald asked.

"Take it," Rob shrugged.

"So we start playing this game we made up. We call it 'Don't Come Any Closer' 'cause we was all playing basketball one night down on Hendee when the police came up and drew on us. We been just trying to have a little fun and, next thing we know, they're down on the ground, and they got their guns aimed at us, yelling 'Don't come any closer,' like we was trying to rush them or something. It was crazy. We didn't do nothin'."

"So Rob had a fight with this girl that night," he continued, "and she called Rob and said she told her brother what Rob said about her and that her brother was coming after us. So we stayed up all night; Kelvin was watching the door. Next day, we left. We just got out of there, man."

Reginald's smile faded suddenly. "Brian Thomas was with us," he said. "He's dead now. Got shot last month; he was only eighteen."

It was something Courtney always dreaded when he saw old friends, finding out who else had died since the last time they'd been together.

Until Reginald and Rob and Kelvin came, there was no one who really understood Courtney's heritage and his homesickness. He didn't know anyone else who'd come there from New Orleans, but he had heard there were Katrina victims who had settled there. One day soon after arriving in Oakland, he had been stopped by a guy in Southland Mall. "Are you from New Orleans?" the man asked him.

"Yeah," Courtney looked at him, but he was no one he recognized.

"I know your face." The man studied him. "Wait a minute. You were the bus driver! I was on that bus that you drove to Lafayette." They talked, and Courtney learned he was one of the men he'd picked up from the Ninth Ward. He'd come out to Oakland to stay with relatives. It felt strange to bump into someone out of the blue who'd shared such a personal experience with him but still remained a stranger.

Courtney felt such a bond with the people who traveled with him on the bus that night, even the ones he didn't know, that it seemed odd not to know what had happened to all of them. He wished he had a crystal ball to see where they all were now.

He wished he had a crystal ball to see into his own future. He knew his commitment would pay off. He was sure God had a plan for his life. In the days since his breakup with Jamie, he'd focused on working hard and playing well. He knew he'd be rewarded by a position on one of the big college teams he dreamed of, and a chance to play in the NBA, but it was up to him to make it happen. Whatever his future held, he'd be able to handle it. He knew how to do without, how to depend on himself in the hardest situation, and how to put his faith in God to take care of him. He would end every day of his college career and beyond in the way he'd ended as a small boy—on his knees asking God for help.

But before his evening prayers each night Courtney sits in the quiet of his apartment looking at a sheet of paper—his R.I.P. list, on which he has written the names of his friends who've died. There are fourteen of them.

Fourteen young men he loved whose memories he tries to honor.

Fourteen young men cut down in gun battles over feuds now forgotten.

Fourteen young men who will never see their dreams.

"Rest in Peace," it says across the top of the paper in large letters. Courtney writes their names in permanent ink on ball caps he wears, on shoes, and on shirts—to remember these friends he has lost as he goes through his day. Many people he knows keep this custom but it's no fad to Courtney. Each name has special meaning. Each time he wears it, he hears the words of his fallen brother in his head.

206

"What are you doing here? Why aren't you out there playing ball?" Ju-Ju would tease every time he saw him. "You gotta play that ball. It's your ticket outta here."

When Pa-Pa heard he'd skipped school again, he said, "Why'd you skip? That's why you can't play ball now——'cause you're in trouble for not going to school like you're s'posed to."

Joe Cash once found him in the breezeway at Fischer shooting dice, "You wastin' your time shootin' dice? You should be shootin' free throws."

Courtney reads his R.I.P. list every night. When he is tired and tempted to slack off, they speak to him. He understands he is their hope for a future. He must make his life count—— for the friends whose names he proudly wears.

When he feels alone, he remembers that they walk with him each step of his journey. He strives to be worthy of their confidence in him and to remember the lessons they taught him.

Whatever he achieves in life will be credited to the boundless blessings he feels God has given him and dedicated to the memory of the friends he has loved and lost. They watch over him as he commits himself, every day, to honoring the sacrifices his grandmother and his mom have made for him and to respecting the memory of the friends who guide his life. Rest in peace, Pa-Pa, Sydney, and Ju-Ju. Rest in peace, Joe Cash, Click, Big Walter, and Henry. Rest in peace, Jeezy, Bug, Fat Black, Woodie, Big Brian, Adris, and Fabe. Rest in peace until the day we all meet again.

Epilogue

Courtney Miles is currently playing basketball at The College of Alameda in Alameda, California.

Jamie Carter has a son. The boy's father is in jail.

Jabbar Gibson is currently serving jail time for drug related charges—and for stealing cars prior to the bus episode.

Gabriel Miles is scheduled to be released from the Louisiana Correctional Institute for Women in late 2010.

Courtney Miles has never gotten a driver's license.

- Still at Alameda
- Jamie's baby daddy is in jail
- Jabbar is in jail
- His mom is released in 2010
- Still has no driver's liscense

[handwritten notes: "+ her story", "Authors story on how she wrote the book"]

Afterword

When my daughter, Emily, a computer technician for the local police department, shared a story she'd heard at a conference of an eighteen-year-old who commandeered a bus after Hurricane Katrina, loaded it with people from the project, and drove it away from New Orleans, I was fascinated, but the idea of writing a book about it seemed far-fetched. How could a white female schoolteacher, old enough to have grown children of my own, become the voice of an eighteen-year-old black man I'd never met? I'd only started writing two years before, had completed a YA novel I was submitting to agents, and was, so far, unpublished.

To complicate matters, I learned that the subject of my story was a basketball star. When someone says "NBA," my English teacher brain thinks "National Book Award." And yet, from the first minute I heard about Courtney Miles, I had to know more. I was spellbound by the story, as powerless to walk away as the Ancient Mariner's wedding guest.

Jabbar Gibson's story was easy to find. He was all over the internet. I was sad to learn he'd wound up in jail. But as I read, I discovered that there were two boys who drove buses that day. From a San Francisco Chronicle article I found online, I learned about Courtney Miles, who was now living in Oakland, California playing basketball.

I had to find him.

It wasn't easy. First, I emailed the writer of the article. Assuming the newspaper had a policy against sharing information about people they'd interviewed, I asked if she might be willing to give Courtney my number in case he was interested in doing a book. Several days passed, and she did not respond.

Next I tried to find a phone number online. Courtney Miles was not listed in Oakland. I was, however, bombarded by offers from dozens of companies that wanted to provide telephone and address information for a small fee—but that seemed kind of creepy. The idea of buying information made me feel like a stalker; I was determined to limit my search to public access information. I went back to the article, found the name of the community college where Courtney played ball, googled the school, and found the basketball coach's email address.

After I wrote to the coach at Courtney's school, I told myself that if I didn't hear from him, I'd drop the whole thing, and I really believe I would have. It was a long shot that the coach would be willing to send me contact information, but this step in the process became a sort of test for me. If this book was meant to be, the information would come. If I didn't hear back, I'd move on to another project.

I will be forever grateful to Coach Justin Labagh . He e-mailed me Courtney's phone number—just one day before my husband, David, and I were already scheduled to leave for San Francisco to visit our friend Doug Grice. I had not visited California in twenty years (and only once before) but fate was sending me within an hour's drive of Courtney Miles, and now I had a way to contact him! I stepped outside the door of my Huntsville, Alabama classroom and dialed his number on my cell phone.

Heart pounding, I tried to rein in my enthusiasm so I didn't come off as some kind of nut case. What words could I use to explain how important he'd become to me without scaring him away? Okay, even I was beginning to wonder if I'd become a bit of a whacko, so preoccupied was I with this idea that wouldn't let me go.

Courtney answered in a soft voice with a Creole accent, and he was understandably guarded when I introduced myself and told him I was interested in talking with him about the possibility of writing a book about him. I held my breath when I asked him if there was already an agreement with another writer to do his story. Amazingly, the answer was no. Courtney agreed to meet me two days later at a McDonald's near his current home in Oakland, California.

The day we first met in California, I introduced myself and barely let him sit down before pouncing with my many questions. My husband reminded me to let him eat his breakfast, so we talked while he ate and I took notes. Courtney was sincere, mature, and soft-spoken, and I felt from the beginning that he was being honest with me. He seemed genuinely humble, and he was very matter-of-fact about his bus rescue. I sensed he had more stories to tell, that the bus trip was just the beginning.

That day I began the year-long process of peeling apart the layers of Courtney Miles' story. At the core were his early years of growing up on his own. From waking up as a seven-year-old on Christmas Eve with a gun in his face to living alone in an abandoned house while in high school, "Streets" had lived a street life I knew little about. I was about to learn.

Some of my education took place in Algiers, Courtney's home just across the Mississippi River from New Orleans. I had agreed to fly him there so we could retrace his bus route, but on the day I was to meet him, he called me in a panic as I was leaving home to drive south. He'd missed his plane. On the way to the Oakland airport, he had been pulled over and detained by the police. They held him just long enough to make him miss his flight for something they said he'd done months before. The "crime"? Eating on the subway. Courtney remembered the incident, but said he'd never received the summons to court they claimed had been mailed to his house.

[handwritten: Cousin died will she interview him]

He made it to the New Orleans airport late that day through some fast talking on both our parts—me by phone to the airlines and him at the ticket counter at the airport. (Thank you, American Airlines.) He was excited about showing me his hometown and introducing me to his grandmother. But then I learned that my introduction to "Miz Geraldine" would have to wait. Her grandson, Courtney's eighteen-year-old cousin, had been gunned down during the night.

A very subdued Courtney told me he wanted to continue our project. I asked him if he was sure he felt up to it, but he said he wanted to go forward with our project. He knew how invested I was, and he'd promised to take me on his journey. As planned, he rode with me to show me the route he'd driven the bus. In my car the cell phone he'd borrowed from a friend rang several times. My lesson for that day went something like this:

-Courtney, why did you answer the phone and then hang up without saying a word?

- *I don't want to talk to people about it, about my cousin. They're trying to say what people are gonna say and stuff. I don't get into all that.*

- So you're just trying to stay out of it, out of your cousin's murder?

- *Yeah. That's why I hung up the phone like that.*

- Did you do something that involves you in the argument that caused the shooting?

- No. It's just your company, you know, who you hang around and stuff. It's not always you. That's why right now, I ain't been hanging with nobody, but because it's my cousin, I'm already in it.

- Is that why you told me we shouldn't get out of the car a little while ago to take a picture of the bus yard?
- Yeah, there was somebody shooting right around there just a little while ago.

- So it could have been people who were looking for you?
- Might have been. I just gotta be honest with you. 'Cause you know, if somethin' happened…

The idea of being drawn into a gang war because of your family is as old as Shakespeare, but it was my first close-up experience with how things worked in Courtney's world. And to be completely honest, I'd always assumed on some level that any young man who was found with a weapon when he was killed had been involved in something he shouldn't have. I learned that plenty of "good" kids who've never been in any trouble carry weapons for protection. If you make good grades and have a clean record, there are always people who want to bring you down. Courtney had no part in the warfare that was threatening to break out; he'd been living in California for months before his cousin's death. But he was in danger, just the same.

Courtney and I had our first and only disagreement when he asked me to help him delay his return flight that weekend to California. He'd already told me his grandmother wanted him to go back to Oakland on schedule; she feared for his safety if he stayed in New Orleans. I told him I wouldn't go against Miz Gerry's instincts, knowing that he could be killed in the conflict that was brewing, and I urged him to return on the flight I'd booked for him earlier.

goes to funeral + visits mom

Instead he tore up his return ticket, stayed for his cousin's funeral, arranged for a brief visit with his mom in jail, and collected enough money from relatives for a bus ticket home. After spending two days and nights on a bus back to California, he called to let me know he'd made it back in time for church on Sunday—and that there were no hard feelings.

I developed a trust in Courtney's judgment and a respect for his resilience. Through many hours of interviews, I began to understand the pressures he faces every day—just trying to stay alive—in addition to studying to pull his grades up, working to improve his basketball game, and never knowing where he'll find money for food. But I have never heard him complain—not once. Instead he thanks God every morning for giving him another day, when so many of his friends have been killed.

Once Courtney decided to trust me, he stayed true to the promise he made me—that he would answer any question I asked him, no matter how hard it was to talk about. My job was to figure out the right questions. Courtney's reserve was part of his survival strategy; the less people knew about his situation, the better. His best defense mechanism had always been to keep to himself, and this barrier was difficult to break through.

Sometimes Courtney withheld information to protect others. After nearly a year of interviews—hours and hours of questions and answers, I got around to asking him about childhood discipline—a question that eventually led to his mother's physical abuse. This was information he didn't want me to have. He loved his mother and he'd hoped to keep this information to himself, but he had promised to tell me the truth. The other piece of information I had to pry from him was the story of his break-up with Jamie, his long-time girlfriend. Again, his silence protected her for as long as he felt he could. Until I finally figured out the right question to ask.

took more than a year to get this information

Telling the truth about two of the three most important women in his life was the hardest part of his work with me. And yet, Courtney needed to tell his story, all of it. We are a culture of storytellers. It's deeply ingrained in our genetic code. We tell stories to try to make sense of traumatic events, to help us cope with the emotional fall-out of their aftermath, and to try to learn from our mistakes so we don't repeat them.

I believe that the story presented here is true. Every scene, every conversation, every thought process has been recreated in the very best way Courtney's memory and my writing could flesh it out. The reconstructed dialogue is the result of months of grilling Courtney and others in an effort to be true to the moment. But it's important to remember that it is the story of the bus trip from Courtney's perspective. In my high school classroom, I reminded my students that Truman Capote called In Cold Blood a "non-fiction novel" because recreating an event on paper is not an exact science. Even our best truth is influenced by our biases and our backgrounds. In spite of all the of notes I've collected from conversations with other people on the bus, relatives in Algiers, friends in California, and basketball coaches, the story that I know is primarily Courtney's.

My husband, David, a criminal defense attorney, is skeptical of "eyewitness" accounts. He's learned in the courtroom that all eyes see differently, all "truths" are biased by our backgrounds and our "baggage." We read with our hearts—not just our eyes—and every story, every song, every painting is interpreted in many different ways. A non-fiction work must account for the fact that life is messy and complicated. There is seldom one truth. There are usually many versions.

Sometimes the pieces of this puzzle formed a picture I hadn't expected, and that may have been true for Courtney, too. When I asked him why his Dad had not been involved in his life until he left for California as a high school senior, he answered, "I can't call it. I don't really know." But as I dug into Courtney's past, I began to understand that the financial resources to support a child were simply not available to him. In an environment where the poor are kept poor because of weak schools, lack of employment, and easy access to drugs, his choices were so much more limited than mine. And he made some bad ones.

Courtney chose to break the cycle of the poverty he was born into. He spent every waking hour honing the athletic skills that were his only ticket to a college education and a bright future. He walked away from the drug culture of the projects, even though his heart was full of gratitude to the people of Fischer who helped raise him.

But he jeopardized it all the day he stole a school bus. He had no idea whether he be arrested or prosecuted or jailed. He knew only that the people he cared most about in the whole world needed his help. They had no way to evacuate the homes that were no longer safe. He found one.

The terrible scenes on my television after Katrina brought back my own memories of being bundled, at age ten, onto a northbound train in New Orleans to return to my home in Coldwater, Mississippi where my Dad, Johnnie Brigman, had taken a job as pastor a few months before. Our visit was cut short by Hurricane Betsy's imminent arrival. My mother, Martha, seven months pregnant, tried to keep a calm face in front of her three children, but the undertone of urgency and danger stays with me to this day.

When Betsy flooded the city, my grandparents evacuated from their tiny DeBore Circle home in Gentilly, but after a couple of days they were determined go home. My grandmother stepped straight from the second floor window of a school building shelter into a boat. "Honey," as my grandfather always called her, was wearing pearls and heels with nylon stockings and clutching her pocketbook. The boat stalled several times—caught on cars underneath the surface of the water. It took them as far as it was able, and they waded the rest of the way home, carrying their belongings over their heads through neck deep water for parts of the journey.

After that one rowboat ride, my grandparents said they weren't leaving again. Purvis Kirkland would stand guard over his yard and his cats for as long as he was able, and Allie declared she would take her chances right there with him. They'd been gone for a good many years when Katrina hit, but when I drove to the old neighborhood and stood in the spongy doorway of the home they once owned, surveying the moldy, rotting interior, I thanked God they didn't live long enough to drown in the deadly surge.

They were plain, honest, hard-working people, my grandparents, and that's another reason I wanted to write this story—to convey what I know about the good people of New Orleans. I grew up with them, and they are some of the smartest, friendliest, warmest and kindest people I know, whether they are black, white, brown, peach or pink. They have been maligned by exaggerated reports of looting by news broadcasters who showed the same two scenes over and over. They have been stereotyped by widespread accounts of rapes, stabbings, and shootings, which could not be substantiated later. They have been accused of being lay-abouts and freeloaders (by people who obviously have not looked for jobs in New Orleans) because they live in government housing. They have been criticized for putting down roots in a city below sea level - by people who've settled in California earthquake zones, Midwest tornado alleys, reclaimed Florida swampland, coastal flood plains and mountainside dwellings all over the country.

They are survivors, and they are heroes. More attention should have been focused on their roles in rescue and recovery efforts after Katrina. The stories are there, on the back pages of the newspapers, stories of fishermen who trolled the toxic flood waters all day and half the night in their own boats, pulling victims aboard, shuttling them to safety, and going back for more. Doctors, nurses, and medical personnel labored in appalling conditions with primitive equipment and limited supplies to save the lives of people dependent on them. Cab drivers combed the streets for disabled victims, construction workers lifted debris off trapped residents with heavy equipment, communications engineers braved the heat and filth to restore radio and cell service to aid in the rescue effort, and kitchen workers salvaged spoiling food from restaurant refrigerators and cooked for hours to feed the hungry homeless. Members of Carnival krewes even hauled in generators used by Mardi Gras floats so they could be hooked up to operate hospitals and police stations.

The people of New Orleans lined up beside the first responders who arrived to help them and said, "What can I do?"

I've spent much of my life among New Orleanians. I love the older women who speak to you on the street and say, "How's ya mama?" in broad river brogues. They've never met my mother but feel it's polite to express general interest in my family. The taxi driver says, "Where ya headed, baby?" like a kind uncle looking after a small child. You ask a man on the street for directions, and he walks you to the corner to make sure you can find your way. The shopkeeper calls, "Hang on a minute, dawlin', ah almos' fuhgot ya lagniappe," and winks as he drops a little something extra into your bag. The people of the Crescent City have a culture all their own and they are true originals. When I was in town for a wedding just two weeks before Katrina, I saw a man walking down St. Philip Street with a cup of coffee—wearing nothing but a bathrobe (open) and penny loafers!

Life, for the working class people of the Big Easy is not always Easy, but it is always Big. They work hard, but they know how to play. They take time to appreciate the simple pleasures of daily living—music, food, spirits, dancing, singing, storytelling, laughing, parading, and cooking. These are Courtney Miles' people, and he is their son.

They are my people too. My history is theirs. My mother and her sisters grew up roller skating around Lee Circle not far from their Coliseum Street duplex. When my grandfather was asked during World War II to leave his post as manager of the A&P store on St. Charles to become the company's traveling auditor, my grandmother stepped up and ran the grocery. My Uncle Charles went to work as a welder at age sixteen for Higgins Shipbuilding Company down at the Industrial Canal. My Uncle Jimmy took the ferry home to Algiers after visiting my Aunt Betty in east New Orleans, walking several miles in lonely morning hours if he stayed too late and missed the last bus. And sadly, a child named Sonny who would have grown up to be my uncle drowned at age eight in Lake Pontchartrain when one of the boots he got for Christmas fell in and he tried to retrieve it. My mother, the unborn child carried in my grandmother's belly to his funeral, is still terrified of the water.

My memories are built on the foundation of my family's Louisiana background. When I was five, my mother would put my sister and me to bed early at our home on Gallier Drive so that she and my dad could type his dissertation for his ThD. degree at the New Orleans Baptist Theological Seminary. His first preaching assignment, in English and in French, was a church at Buras-Triumph, the tiny community where Katrina would later make landfall. My mom rode the bus every day to her secretarial job at an insurance agency just off Canal Street to put my dad through school, and he took care of us after daycare, reading us the books that sparked my life-long love of language.

We had no money for extras, but none was needed for a childhood in an enchanted city. We had Storyland in City Park, the Mardi Gras fountain down at the Lakefront, Mr. Bingle at Maison Blanche, Audubon Zoo's Monkey Hill, and the bakery in the garage behind a house on Verbena that made hot doughnuts mere words can't describe. I ate cake at birthday parties held on streetcars, slurped Old Fashioned Nectar Crème sno-balls topped with condensed milk in summers, dug for plastic baby dolls in King Cakes, and ate hot fudge sundaes in my pajamas in our cozy red Chevrolet Corvair, its interior bathed in the yellow glow of Zesto that lit the soft night. We saved our change for rare outings to Pontchartrain Beach's amusement park where we had our picture made in the clown's mouth, watched high-wire acts, and dared each other to ride the Wild Maus.

As a teenager I shopped at D.H. Holmes ("Holmes's") and K & B Drug Store ("K.B.'s") and strolled the French Quarter, usually under the watchful eyes of my beloved Aunt Ev and Uncle Norman, the Cooks who treated me like their own. My sister Julie and cousin Carolyn and I giggled over beignets at Café du Monde until we were covered in powdered sugar. And when Uncle Norman caught us peeking in the open doors of the strip clubs on Bourbon Street, he told us to go right ahead. He said my daddy, the preacher, told me how it ought to be and it was his job to show me how it really was.

Mardi Gras was always, is still, and will forever be the most magical time of the year. When a masked man on a lighted float called my mother's name and handed down an armload of glittering jewels, I began to see her in a new light. To this day she does not know who her secret admirer was—the mystique of the masquerade. I still love the drama of the biggest night parades— Bacchus and Endymion. For weeks beforehand, I save one-dollar bills to hand off to the flambeaux carriers who continue the tradition. I want them to be there—still twirling, dipping, and dancing under heavy iron torches that drip liquid fire—when I bring grandchildren one day to Carnival, my forever favorite fete.

We preacher's kids move around a lot, so I've lived in many locations from Louisiana to Mississippi to Alabama. But New Orleans will always be my home.

Home for Courtney these days is Oakland, California, far away from his Louisiana roots. He has exemplified his motto of "Get in where you fit in," with grace and dignity, embracing each new experience with a glad heart and willing spirit. Throughout the process of writing this book, he has inspired me with his optimism and his deep faith in God. My life has been enriched and uplifted by his example and his friendship. Whatever path he chooses in life and wherever he makes his home, he will be a blessing to those around him.

Acknowledgments

Many thanks to Emily Elam for the story inspiration and warm encouragement for this book, to Drew McDowell for fabulous artwork and good company on the route retracing trip, Julie Moreau for thoughtful edits and input, to Tommy Siniard for the compelling title, and to Susan Siniard for her faith in me and for cheering me on—always.

Alex Glass, my agent, believed in this story from the beginning; he is a man of insight, intelligence, and—in our humble opinion—impeccable taste. And no writer could ask for more talented and generous hometown mentors than R.A. Nelson (*Teach Me, Breathe My Name, Days of Little Texas,* and *Throat*) and Hester Bass (*The Secret World of Walter Anderson*), who've offered invaluable advice, encouragement, and support that kept me moving forward.

Thanks also to friends who read and/or nurtured: Doug Grice, Hannah Cail, Geoff Evans, Megan Mercier, Ben Morehead, Michael Walker, Andrew Cotten, Jim Sherwood, Jerry Whitworth, Shaw Bowman, Beth Thames, Walter Thames, Mike Chappell, Raymond Harrell, Michael Patton, Alice Evans, Wendy Stephens, Betsy Howard, Gordon Maples, Lula Mae Martin, Winnie Boyd,

Betty Hopper, Bryan Thames, and Russell Goldfinger. Also to all my wonderful Huntsville High students whose enthusiasm for my writing was genuine and much appreciated.

Most importantly, David McDowell guides and supports everything I do with amazing instincts, a huge heart, and more love and patience than I can ever hope to deserve.

And there is no way I can adequately express my appreciation to my parents, Johnnie and Martha Brigman.

He gave me poetry and she gave me power.

I love you, Mom.

Dad, you are missed more than words can ever, ever say.

Good Books:

- *Breach of Faith: Hurricane Katrina and the Near Death of a Great American City* by Jed Horne

- *Zeitoun* by Dave Eggers

- *Rising Tide: The Great Mississippi Flood of 1927 and How It Changed America* by John M. Barry

- *1 Dead in Attic: After Katrina* by Chris Rose

Reading Group Discussion/Teacher's Guide

Before You Read

1. Discuss any stories you've heard about Hurricane Katrina.

2. Look at a map of the New Orleans area and find the location of Algiers across the Mississippi River.

3. Define the term situational ethics. Is there any circumstance in which stealing something that doesn't belong to you could be justified, or is it always wrong to steal, no matter what? Imagine various scenarios in which it might be difficult to make a decision about taking something that could help others.

Individual Research

Find blogs online written by survivors of Hurricane Katrina and summarize the information you find about their personal accounts of their experiences.

Journal Writing

If you had only five minutes to pack before a major natural disaster and could only take one suitcase, what would you pack? Make a list in priority order.

Chapter 1 – Prelude to Disaster

Tuesday, August 23

1. List three things we learn about Courtney's physical description in Chapter 1.

2. What evidence do we have of Courtney's commitment to basketball? his talent?

Wednesday, August 24

3. Why does the author include a scene of extreme violence so early in the book?

4. What is the effect of the narrative shift to present tense?

5. What do you think Miz Geraldine means by "Follow your first mind."? Is it good advice? Why or why not?

Thursday, August 25

6. What is Courtney's nickname and where did he get it?

7. Why does Courtney consider the people of Fischer his family?

8. What two physical displays show his allegiance to his neighborhood?

9. How did Courtney stay away from the street gangs? Why was it hard?

10. What does Courtney fear when he jokes with the street dudes? Why?

Friday, August 26

11. What are three names Courtney calls his grandmother? Explain them.

12. Why didn't Courtney take the meteorologist's hurricane warnings seriously?

13. What were the names of two previous hurricanes that damaged New Orleans?

Chapter 2 – Riding Out the Storm

1. List several words and phrases that help set the mood and establish tone.

2. In Shakespeare's plays, a storm in the opening scene symbolizes chaos in the political or social world. What trauma has Courtney suffered that might be seen as a parallel to weather in Chapter 2?

3. List some of the similes and metaphors used to describe the scene outside.

4. List three other phrases that describe Algiers after Katrina.

226

Journal Writing

Write about a time when you didn't take something seriously that later turned out to be a bigger deal than you thought.

Chapter 3 –When the Levees Fail

1. What is a levee? How is it made?

2. List five things that contributed to the flooding of New Orleans.

3. What historical evidence shows Algiers' higher elevation than New Orleans?

Chapter 4 – This Time is Different

1. How does the other boys' treatment of Courtney indicate his status as a leader?

2. Why was Courtney calmer about the post-flood problems than most people?

3. Is their anger over water bottles dropped from planes justified? Why or why not?

4. What health dangers did the people of Fischer Projects face?

5. Why couldn't the people walk out of the city?

Chapter 5 – The Key to Escape

1. What is the median called in New Orleans? Why? Are there regional names for things in your city a visitor might not understand?

2. List three obstacles to the stealing of the bus that might have stopped someone less determined.

Journal Writing

Write about a time when you tried to accomplish something that was difficult. What were the obstacles that stood in your way and how did you overcome them?

Chapter 6 – Drive

1. Discuss possible multiple meanings of the title of the chapter.

2. What do we learn that complicates Courtney's decision to take the bus?

3. As they drive out of the lot, Courtney admits he never really thought they'd find buses with keys and gas. Why did he go to the bus lot if he felt that way?

Journal Writing

Write about a time something happened that you hoped for but didn't really expect.

Chapter 7 – Loaded

1. Why did the people of Fischer project feel the government had abandoned them?

2. Where does Algiers, Louisiana's name come from?

3. Besides the lack of funds for transportation and shelter, list two other reasons the people of Fischer didn't evacuate before the hurricane.

Chapter 8 – Roadblock

1. What memory is triggered by passing his old elementary school? Why is this important to the story?

2. Why is it ironic that his mother's drug money keeps him healthy?

3. Courtney relies on instinct, doing what he <u>feels</u> is right even more often than what he <u>thinks</u> is right. Can you think of a time when you relied on instinct to make an important decision? Did it work out well? Why or why not?

4. What was Courtney's plan for the passengers on his bus as they pulled onto the Westbank Expressway and headed out of town?

Journal Writing

Reread the author's description of Courtney's fear as he drives away from the police roadblock. Write about a time when you were afraid, paying special attention to your description of how fear feels to you. Include physical reactions as well as emotional ones.

Chapter 9 - To Lafayette

1. What metaphor is used to describe the landscape?

2. List two similes used to describe the randomness of the devastation. How is the second one extended into the next sentence?

3. What flashback is triggered by Courtney's concern for people left homeless by the storm?

4. What fantasy does Courtney indulge in while living alone in the empty house?

5. Why does his Grandmother say his mom stops calling him? Do you agree and how do you feel about it?

Journal Writing

About his mother, the author says, "Courtney loved her and wanted her to be happy. But he didn't know how to help her." Write a journal about a time when you wanted to help someone but had trouble finding a way.

Chapter 10 - Ninth Ward Survivors

1. Why are the Ninth Ward victims' stories so different from the stories of the Algiers people?

2. List some of the substances that contaminated the flood waters, posing health risks to the residents forced to flee in them.

3. Why were numbers of dead painted on houses with spray paint?

4. What were some of the problems faced by police officers after the storm?

5. What rumor fueled cries of racism by residents of flooded areas? What two factors influenced the rumor's spread?

6. How did some reporters treat stories about white and black victims differently?

7. Many New Orleans victims were offended at being called refugees? Why?

8. Why does Courtney feel lonely on the bus?

9. What are some of the things he worries about while driving? Which do you think are the most valid concerns?

Journal Writing

Write about a time when you felt lonely.

Chapter 11 – Promises to Keep

1. Why does Courtney park on the side street at the Cajundome?

2. Why does Courtney step forward to answer the man's questions?

3. Why does he walk to the front of the line when they first arrive?

4. What two sports similes are used in this chapter?

5. Describe Grandma Streets' reaction to Courtney's story? What does this say about her?

6. Why does he go with his Dad to the football game after hiding at his Grandmother's?

7. What poem do the titles of Chapter 10 and 11 come from? What promises does Courtney set out to keep at the end of Chapter 10?

Journal Writing

Write about a time when you had to tell a parent, relative, or friend about something you'd done that might get you in trouble. How did you break the news and what was the reaction?

Chapter 12 – Miles to Go Before I Sleep

1. What do we learn about Courtney's mom? Describe the two sides of her Gemini personality. What factors might contribute to the "rages" that came over her?

2. How does Courtney try to justify her behavior?

3. What does Courtney do to try to help his mother?

4. How did Hurricane Katrina hurt Courtney's chance to pursue his dreams?

5. In your opinion, why do the two National Guardsmen allow Courtney to drive back into the city when they're under orders to keep people out.

Journal Writing

Write about a time when someone you loved or respected disappointed you.

Chapter 13 – The Cajundome

1. What do Courtney and Tom learn about the fate of the people on the second bus?

2. What were conditions like in the Cajundome?

Journal Writing

Write about a time when your living conditions were not what you expected. How did you cope with the situation?

Chapter 14 – FEMA Trailer

1. Describe the FEMA trailer Courtney and his grandmother are given as temporary housing. What is their reaction to their living conditions?

2. What does Courtney's grandmother plan to try to get back to normal?

3. Courtney realizes as he goes to enroll at Northside that he will never see many of his friends again. If you knew you might not see your friends tomorrow, what things would you want to do and say today?

4. Describe Coach Moore. What techniques does he use to motivate his players? How do you feel about him?

Journal Writing

Courtney is expelled from school for something he says he didn't do. Write about a time when you were falsely accused or someone you know was falsely accused.

Chapter 15 – Get In Where You Fit In

1. How does the situation change at the high school after Courtney plays ball on Open Gym night?

2. Why didn't people try to fix up their homes after the storm?

3. Why is Courtney not allowed to play ball at Helen Cox High School?

4. What offer comes from Gil Dorsey-Wagner? How did he know about Courtney?

5. In what way does Courtney's decision to move to California parallel his invitation to people on the bus to "get in where you fit in"?

Journal Writing

Courtney feels alive for the first time in weeks when he Plays ball. Describe something you love doing and tell how it makes you feel.

Chapter 16 – Oakland

1. What were some of Courtney's concerns as he flew to Oakland?

2. Who does Courtney meet in the office of the Castlemont? Why is he surprised?

3. Why does Courtney have such a hard time academically at Castlemont?

4. How did other people in Oakland step in to help him succeed? Why did they?

Journal Writing

Write about a time when other people helped you accomplish something important.

Chapter 17 – A College Education

1. What adjustments did Courtney have to make at City College?

2. What insights does Courtney have about his father?

3. Describe Courtney's tattoo and explain what it represents.

4. How does the marijuana incident make you feel about Courtney?

Journal Writing

Make a list of expectations you have about college. What aspects do you expect to be difficult and what will you enjoy?

Chapter 18 – Alone Again

1. What is the devastating news Courtney learns about Jamie ? How does he take it?

2. Why doesn't the author reveal Courtney's conversation with Jamie after he learns that she's betrayed him? How do you feel about that?

3. What does Courtney do to relieve his pain?

4. What is Courtney's RIP list? Why does he keep it?

Journal Writing

Make a list of things you do to lift your spirits when you're feeling down.

Extra Journal Writing Assignments

Write about people in your life who have functioned in parental roles who are not your biological parents.

Write about a time when you were tempted to join in an activity that you knew was wrong. How did you handle the situation?

Write about a time someone gave you good advice. Explain how you applied it and how it helped you in life.

Write about a time when you or someone you know performed a heroic deed.

Made in the USA
Lexington, KY
08 June 2017